CHINA IN THE 1980s

SCANDINAVIAN INSTITUTE OF ASIAN STUDIES

STUDIES ON ASIAN TOPICS

STUDIES ON ASIAN TOPICS NO. 9

CHINA IN THE 1980s –
AND BEYOND

Edited by
BIRTHE ARENDRUP
CARSTEN BOYER THØGERSEN
ANNE WEDELL-WEDELLSBORG

CURZON PRESS

SCANDINAVIAN INSTITUTE OF ASIAN STUDIES
Kejsergade 2, DK-1155 Copenhagen K

First published 1986
Curzon Press Ltd: London and Malmö
© SIAS Copenhagen 1986

ISBN
0 7007 0174 5
ISSN
0142 6028

Printed in Great Britain by
Nene Litho, Irthlingborough, Northants.
Bound by Woolnough Bookbinding, Irthlingborough, Northants.

CONTENTS

EDITORS

Birthe Arendrup, East Asian Institute, University of Copenhagen.

Carsten Boyer Thøgersen, Institute of East Asian Studies, University of Aarhus.

Anne Wedell-Wedellsborg, Institute of East Asian Studies, University of Aarhus.

CONTRIBUTORS

Marianne Bastid, Research Professor, Centre national de la recherche scientifique, Paris.

Christoph Harbsmeier, Professor, Østasiatisk Institutt, Universitet i Oslo.

Giorgio Mantici, Research Fellow, Istituto Universitario Orientale, Napoli.

Detlef Rehn, Research Fellow, Ostasien-Institut, Bonn.

Tony Saich, Assistant Professor, Sinologisch Instituut, Rijksuniversiteit Leiden.

E.B. Vermeer, Assistant Professor, Sinologisch Instituut, Rijksuniversiteit Leiden.

PREFACE

The Sandbjerg Symposium *China in the 1980s - and Beyond: Political, Economic and Cultural Perspectives* took place on 5th to 8th of November 1982 at the Sandbjerg Castle in the south of Jutland.

The Symposium was jointly arranged by the Scandinavian Institute of Asian Studies, Copenhagen, the East Asian Institute, University of Copenhagen and the Institute of East Asian Studies, University of Aarhus. The Symposium was mainly directed towards contemporary and future developments in China, the idea being to get a comprehensive view of the present tendencies within various aspects of Chinese society.

At a previous symposium in 1978 arranged by the Institute of East Asian Studies, University of Aarhus, Danish and other Scandinavian scholars on contemporary China had the opportunity to give lectures. This time the arranging institutions especially wanted to include other European scholars, thus providing the chance to listen and to exchange views. Indeed, the facilities at the Sandbjerg Castle made this possible during the three days of being together.

The Sandbjerg Symposium and the publication of this volume were made possible by grants from the Danish Research Council for the Humanities, the Danish Ministry of Education, the Knud Højgaard Foundation and Superfos Ltd. We are grateful to these Institutions for their generous support.

The Editors

INTRODUCTION:
A LEAP INTO THE TWENTY-FIRST CENTURY

The profile of China in the 1980s started to emerge in
December 1978 at the Third Plenum of the 11th Party Congress
of the Chinese Communist Party. It was then that Party Vice-
Chairman Deng Xiaoping seized power. In just over two years
he would have successfully outmanoeuvred Hua Guofeng, de-
priving him of both the Premiership and the post of CPC
Chairman. This allowed him to begin to realize some of the
plans for his vision of a modernized China which he had
nurtured for two decades whilst in the shadow of Mao Zedong.
   In this respect, one can talk of a process of liberation
taking place in China. Deng Xiaoping, supported by a wave of
popular feeling, has managed to reverse the feudal-socialist
'Mao-Cult' which had emerged since the Cultural Revolution.
This accomplished, China was ready for change. Whilst the
patriotic perspective of Deng's political thought has never
been in doubt, some foreign observers have recently posed the
question 'Is Deng Xiaoping leading China away from Socialism?'
What has happened, in fact, is that the Cultural Revolutionaries' effort to create equality and socialism by using the
superstructure has been rejected, and replaced by the traditional socialist approach of promoting socialism by developing the productive forces. So in answer to the question of
how to develop socialism in China, one may still point to the
present manifestation and realization of a socialist modernized China - now in Dengist style.
   In the past six years, China has undergone profound changes
in its organization, economy and politics. Any investigation
of this period, therefore, must include a consideration of the
rôle of continuity and change with respect to earlier policies
and those policies which will guide China into the twenty-
first century.
   The Dengist modernization of China will, of course, build
upon the social structures established over the twenty years
of Maoist policy. On the other hand, though Chinese leaders
are consciously aware of the treatment China received at the
hands of foreign powers in the hundred years leading up to
1949 they have opened the door to the international market in
an attempt to eradicate internal feudal structures and 'catch-
up' with the rest of the world. In the opinion of the Chinese
leaders this can be done on China's own terms. The door is
open for the time being - but could, quite possibly, be closed
again.
   In addition to the current internal re-orientation, China
is experiencing another kind of social upheaval in learning to
cope with the adoption of foreign technological and managerial
practices. These, although well-known and practised in

industrialized countries, have yet to be tried and tested in
the Chinese context.

This process recalls some older chapters of China's
history whilst more recent ones appear more distant. Thus,
the last twenty years of a two-line-struggle are missing.
Present today is the national ambition for China to assume an
economic and political position in world affairs commensurate
with its size and history. This makes one recall Kang Youwei
and his abortive, but perspective attempt to reform China
almost one hundred years ago.

Deng Xiaoping's efforts to take advantage of China's
opportunity for rapid modernization have emphasized development of productive forces through a combination of economic
stimuli and so-called 'objective economic laws'. This can be
seen in the implementation of a rural policy based on the
contract system of responsibility for production, and the
stressing of material incentives in the extension of decision-
making powers for enterprises, combined with the utilization
of the world market for new technology and foreign investment
mentioned earlier.

At present, the central role of the party has not been
questioned, but this state of affairs cannot be certain to
last. While Mao sought to spur the development of the productive forces by revolutionizing the superstructure (his own
personal command of the party being one important exception),
Deng has concentrated on the rapid development of the productive forces without attempting to change the structure of
the party accordingly. The repercussions of China's changing
internal economy and its contact with the outside world will -
sooner or later - necessitate a re-assessment of the status of
a centralized communist party in China. Meanwhile, apart from
some minor re-organization within the party like the establishment of an Advisory Commission and a Commission for
Discipline Inspection - primarily to create some bodies the
chairmanship of which would be held by the senior veterans
Deng Xiaoping and Chen Yun - basically nothing has been
changed in regard to the fundamental concept of the role of
the party. Rooted in the tradition of a Leninist party this
question does not seem to have been one of Deng's primary
concerns.

Since the introduction of the Agricultural Production
Responsibility System in 1979 and the decision of the Central
Committee of the CPC in September 1980 to implement the new
agricultural policy, China has not only witnessed a radical
de-collectivization but also the beginning of a new developmental cycle. The de-collectivization has changed one
important part of the existing political system and will soon
raise demands for a further revision of the political system
as such. Political and administrative decision-making has
been removed from the People's Communes to the newly-

2

established Township Governments. Now, instead of communes, regional co-operatives and enterprises have been set up within the limits of production brigades. Together with small family industrial undertakings, the existing commune and brigade enterprises will retain their individual economic functions and are regarded as the mainstay of rural economy.

The gradual concentration of land among efficient farming families has resulted in a widespread and acknowledged disparity in income. In this respect one might change Deng Xiaoping's saying: 'It doesn't matter if a cat is black or white; if it catches mice it is a good cat', to 'It doesn't matter which cats catch the mice, only that the mice are caught'. As long as some peasant cats are getting fat - catching the opportunities for economic development - it is all right. Thus, the disparity in incomes is seen merely as an encouragement for those peasants less better off to do a better job. Then, if they remain unsuccessful for some reason, the peasants have the opportunity of becoming hired workers in the rural industries: into which the specialized household's thriving entrepreneurship is supposed to develop in the near future.

Evidently, the new rural policy is benefiting from some short-term gains inherent in the departure from the former collective structure. This has led to the first substantial increases in income for Chinese peasants since the 1950s. This surplus income has been used mainly for consumption and construction of housing accommodation rather than for other types of investment. In addition to the rise in the demand for consumer goods, there has also been an increased need for an expansion of services in the countryside, especially those related to farming. The households engaged in farming being primarily small still, they cannot provide all the resources needed for efficient farming. In so far as the surplus income is invested in establishing new enterprises - financed by individuals, former collective structures, or a mixture of both - then a new means of organizing small handicrafts, light industry, services, shops and marketing corporations is being established. This will again exert pressure for a further diversification of labour: thus absorbing some of the surplus labour from agriculture. But the long-term success of this policy still depends on whether it proves to be possible to transfer the surplus rural labour force to other employment areas.

The prospects for the future being outlined in the rural areas is that of expanding small-scale industry and service trades primarily employing the unfortunate peasants who have given up farming and moved to the rural cities. The reduced number of peasants engaged in agriculture and related activities will be those who in these years, for various reasons,

get a flying start along with successful co-operative organizations. The agricultural policies have been implemented
for economic reasons: apparently without giving much thought
to the resulting changes in the political structure. The
diversification of labour together with the number of new
professions will create their own new social structure. If
these new social groups - like agricultural producers' associ-
ations with the right to promote their special interests or
the vast groups of rural workers in different trades - get
frustrated in their demands on the political system, they
might seek other ways to promote their demands. Thus a whole
new class structure will emerge in the countryside.

Another problem that will arise in the foreseeable future
is that the decline in capital expenditure will be difficult
to reverse if steps are not taken to promote investment.
Also, the decline in the collective funding of social services
has meant that access to education and medical care has become
increasingly dependent on family income. These points beg the
question of how far the observation of 'objective economic
laws' in the pursuit of modernization will be allowed to
polarize China socially?

In due time, the peasants may be expected to demand larger
working units in order to rationalize their farming methods.
How such units are to be formed, though, is still not certain.
The land formally remains in the possession of the collective
and, while this is still the case, it will continue to be
possible to talk of socialism. But it is questionable for
how long this formality will remain feasible in practice.

The establishment of the Special Economic Zones has been
another spectacular decision of the Deng Administration. The
official explanation for introducing the zones was to
accelerate the growth of capital-intensive high technology,
the benefits of which China needed but could not afford. The
economic basis of the zones is capitalist - or 'market mechanism' as it is officially termed. Other fields - such as
science, education, culture and tourism - however, are being
developed along socialist and patriotic lines. Thus, one
paradox of the zones is that they represent the construction
of an economic system based on capitalism alongside a pro-
claimed socialist ideology.

When seen in the light of their original intentions, the
Special Economic Zones can hardly be claimed to have been a
success. Having failed to attract technology-intensive
investment from the US, Japan and Western Europe, what little
investment has taken place has been Hongkong and overseas
Chinese capital. Another of the goals originally set was that
the zones should act as buffers - or filters - between the
Chinese socialist system and the capitalist world outside.
This would, also, give the Beijing economic planners an

4

opportunity to experiment with and examine the mechanisms of
a market economy, providing them with a working 'laboratory'
for adapting a capitalist model to Chinese economic and
social conditions. Further, in the case of Shenzhen, a
secondary aim might have been to prepare the ground for the
taking-over of Hongkong in 1997 by initiating a semi-
capitalist region of China with which Hongkong could, eventually, be integrated.

The Special Economic Zones were initially established on a
trial basis and, although they have not, as yet, fulfilled
their initial economic purpose, the concept of investment
zones has become an important part of China's modernization
programme and has spread, in various forms, to a number of
coastal and inland cities. What is noticeable generally,
though, is that while the central authorities have the last
word with regard to the size of foreign capital investment
in these zones, the principle of decentralization in economic
matters is indisputably clear: strengthening regional
economic pluralism and reviving the old contradictions between cities and countryside and between coastal and inland
areas.

This trend of encouraging economic pluralism is evident
within industrial policies too. The reform of the urban
economic structure is aimed at a separation of the functions
of government from those of the enterprises, giving the
enterprises greater freedom of self-management and establishing a close link between profits and workers' wages via
increased productivity incentives in the 'economic responsibility systems'. In a new management policy, the managing
director in any project assumes full responsibility for the
production, management and operation of his enterprise.

The above measures are designed to encourage production.
This will enhance the industrial output in the short term.
But competition and inequality between enterprises will
increase. In order to avoid economic irrationalities caused
by competition, a balance is said to be being established
between the central planning and the market. The necessity
of in-depth reform of the economic structure is given predominance in this policy, but the impact of the reforms on
the political system is hardly mentioned, except for the
message that party members are expected to support the new
policies.

Perhaps it has been in the sphere of ideology that Deng
Xiaoping met his greatest challenge. In the period of re-
appraisal which followed the Cultural Revolution, the
Chinese people was said to have suffered the 'ten evil years'
at the hands of the CPC under Chairman Mao. Yet the re-
evaluation of the role of both Mao and the CPC had to be a
positive one; partly out of consideration for the continuity
of the CPC's power monopoly, and partly because the ideology

of the CPC is so synonymous with Mao Zedong who had been chairman for more than 40 years. In approaching this para-dox Deng was able to display all the political skill he had acquired during a lifelong membership of the CPC.

The publication in 1983 of *The Selected Works of Deng Xiaoping from 1975-1982* revealed very clearly Deng's re-flections whilst he prepared for his ideological showdown with twenty years of Maoist policy. In a practical, down-to-earth style he weighed the pros and cons: a Resolution on the history of the Party had to be written. Within the party there was an urgent demand for the record to be set straight. Originally, the Resolution was only concerned with the history of the party after 1949. This posed the problem that an appraisal of Mao's contribution would seem disproportionately negative: Mao's errors of judgement coming predominantly in the period after 1958. Then, at the suggestion of Chen Yun, Deng decided to include the period before 1949 - giving Mao's contributions more predominance which, in turn, left room for a critique of Maoist policies after 1958.

The result of this has been the establishment of the 'Mao Zedong-Thought System'. This is not necessarily identical to Mao's political ideas and it became possible to argue that Mao Zedong's mistakes were merely misunderstandings by Mao of the 'Mao Zedong-Thought System'. Deng's contribution, then, had been to re-establish the original 'Mao Zedong-Thought System', incorporating within this framework the four basic socialist priciples he had laid down some years earlier: support for the Socialist Road; the People's Demo-cratic Dictatorship; leadership by the Communist Party and Marxism-Leninism-Mao Zedong Thought.

Though Deng managed to resolve this ideological up-dating quite elegantly, he has consistently displayed little intention to reconcile the current changes in the economic sphere with the functions of the party. Deng's sole objec-tive seems to have been to create a new official ideology consistent with China's long revolutionary history essential to a communist - or any - ruling party.

Since 1979, efforts have been made within China to facilitate the take-over of Hongkong in 1997 and improve economic relations with overseas Chinese communities. Ideo-logical questions have received less prominence and a rapid economic modernization by all available means has been stressed.

Deng Xiaoping's reform policy does not seem to constitute an interlude in China's twentieth-century history. On the contrary, the 1980s will see the foundations being laid for China's leap into the status of a Newly Industrialized Country - in somewhat the same way as Mexico or Argentina.

INTRODUCTION

Deng has lit the fuses of a host of contradictions present
in Chinese society which - initially, at least - is
benefiting from the dynamism and energy inherent in these
contradictions. Ultimately, these contradictions will
produce change. What kind of change remains to be seen,
but change is inevitable. It is also certain that, in this
process, China's social structures will be changed more
radically than they have been in the past 30 years; a new
balance in the class structure will emerge, probably giving
rise to social conflicts of a different - but not less
violent - nature than those of the Cultural Revolution.

Carsten Boyer Thøgersen

EDUCATION, YOUTH AND SOCIAL PERSPECTIVES IN THE EARLY 1980s

Marianne Bastid

Editors' Introduction

Two main issues are shown to be the present focus of concern as regards schooling and higher education in China. One is the necessity of ensuring highly qualified personnel, the other that of ensuring the professional and social integration of the young generation. Government policies on the former issue have resulted in only a slight increase in the rate of enrolment into universities and technical colleges, while efforts to improve the quality and organization of teaching have proved quite effective. To the latter issue, involving problems of unemployment and moral crises among the young, the remedies applied have been the introduction of structural reforms of the educational system and the reinforcement of ideological work and political instruction. In the second part of her article, Marianne Bastid discusses the society outlined by the present educational measures and the popular reactions it may be expected to provoke.

Youth education is not an issue unique to China. But its particular importance in China lies firstly in the fact that it involves the world's largest figures: 205 million people now in school and nearly three-fifths of the total population under twenty-five years of age.[1] Moreover, ten years of Cultural Revolution and political turmoil have so deeply shaken existing values, beliefs and institutions, that the rebuilding of the educational system stands as a kind of test of what still remains from the past, and of what may be the new concerns in Chinese society, its purposes and its perceptions of its own future.

It would indeed be misleading to consider any educational system as a faithful mirror of social hierarchies, interests and goals, since schooling brings into play many interacting factors that can determine the survival of old patterns of behaviour or the early introduction of new ones which do not fit prevailing concepts or values in other segments of society. However, the main ideas and values embodied in an educational system are shared at least by those who establish it, and the youth undergoing education under that system are bound to be influenced by it in some ways, so

that an examination of educational policy has significant
relevance to the assessment of a society's evolution and
prospects.

An investigation into recent Chinese educational debates
and reform measures will help in the analysis of the con-
crete tasks assigned to school education in the China of
1982, and of the means adopted to fulfil them. When further
light is cast on the blueprint for social organization and
social relations which underlie the current educational
system, then one can assess its chances for becoming the
actual pattern of Chinese society.

CHINESE ASSESSMENT OF ISSUES AND THEIR SOLUTIONS

As opposed to criticism and policies in the past, recent
discussions and reforms of education are confined to functional aspects of the system. Whether in views expressed
by the public or by official statements, the tasks assigned
to school education focus on two main issues. One is the
need to train very highly qualified personnel, the other is
to insure the professional and social integration of the
younger generation. There is general agreement that in the
past the training provided by the educational system has
been of inadequate quality and has been available to insufficient numbers of young people.

The State: Lack of Qualified Personnel

As regards the first issue – the training of highly qualified personnel – there is indeed strong pressure to increase
enrolment in specialized fields and higher education. Such
pressure on the part of the public and some official
quarters argues on economic grounds, stressing the low
figures for qualified technical leadership. As a matter of
fact, in 1980 China could boast only 6 million scientific
and technical workers, a number which according to the pro-
visions of Chinese planners back in 1960 was the objective
that should have been reached in 1967 to meet national
requirements.[2] By 1979 research workers numbered just
310,000, while the year before, Fang Yi, head of the Commission for Science and Technology, had stated that 800,000
would be needed in 1985.[3] However, although seldom expressed publicly, social motivations also lay behind the
urgent drive to open up access to high-level training.
Increasing enrolment would mean more 'iron-bowls' available,
that is more opportunities for prestigious, secure and

relatively well-paid jobs, since at this level employment
together with state-cadre status is automatically provided
by the government. It is bitterly felt that the rate of
recruitment in universities and technical colleges provides
too few opportunities for legitimate social expectations.
   This demand for widening the access to highly-qualified
training has met as yet with little response. The plan
adopted in 1980 provided for a gradual increase in university enrolment: the entrance quota was to exceed 300,000 in
1982, to reach 400,000 in 1984 and 700,000 in 1990.[4] But
the actual quota in 1982 has been only 300,000,[5] that is
less than 10 per cent more than the average in the last few
years, and the revised draft of the sixth five-year plan
for 1981-1985 sets a quota of 400,000 for 1985 only.[6] It
should be noted anyway that the increase will coincide with
the coming of age of the greatly increased number of individuals born in the 1966-1974 period, so that it can bring
very little relief as regards social expectations.
   The annual enrolment of research students (*yanjiusheng*)
has declined from 10,708 in 1978 to 3,620 in 1980.[7] It
reached 11,000 in 1982, but will still not exceed 20,000 in
1985.[8] Increasing from 420 to 900 in 1983, the quota of
doctoral candidates (*gongdu boshi xuewei*) hardly opens up
larger avenues.[9] Studies abroad could provide some further
opportunities. But it does not seem that high-level
training through this channel is going to reach significant
numbers of young people. According to the statistics of
the Ministry of Education, from 1978 to the end of June
1982 some 12,000 students and scholars were sent to study
abroad.[10] Most of them, however, were visiting scholars:
the figures available for 1978-1980 show that only 673 were
regular students attending an institution of higher
learning, and 619 were enrolled in a postgraduate programme.[11] In 1983, 1,000 should be selected for enrolment
in postgraduate programmes abroad.[12] Even with the
addition of those who manage to study in foreign countries
at their own expense through family connections, it is not
likely that more than a few thousand will get full training
abroad each year.
   Enrolment increase is more conspicuous in secondary
technical schools (*zhongdeng jishu xuexiao*) where graduates
are also given employment by the government with access to
the cadre status. It rose from around 100,000 a year in
1977 to 251,000 in 1979, but has since remained steady.[13]
   It should be stressed that such small quotas for higher
and technical education not only put severe limits on
social expectations but also reveal a rather modest perspective as regards economic development. For the time

being supplementary adult middle and higher technical training programmes enrol only some 300,000 people every year.[14]

On the issue of highly qualified training, government policies have more efficiently met public demand as regards the improvement in quality. Serious attention has been paid to renovating the teaching staff. Older, more experienced and better trained teachers discarded on political grounds during the Cultural Revolution, and some of them since the anti-rightist movement of 1957, have been put in charge of fundamental courses and given the leading part in the supervision of teaching. Meanwhile their younger colleagues enlisted since 1966 have been requested to attend special intensive courses and have been either confirmed in their position or promoted or transferred to other tasks according to their performances in special examinations conducted by each institution in the case of higher education, and by local authorities as regards primary and secondary school teachers. Various devices aimed at the permanent professional improvement of the teaching staff have been introduced: new schedule regulations providing a minimum time for personal reading and the preparation of lectures, a revival of the publication of learned journals, special lectures and refresher courses, academic symposia, competitive examinations for scholarships abroad or research positions.

In addition to such *ad hoc* measures which have also been used in the past, some institutional reforms of more far-reaching consequences have been adopted. They concern the organization of teaching. They include the restoration of a priority or key schools system (*zhongdian xuexiao*), a creation of the nationalist government back in the 1930s, which had already been in force in the early 1950s and 1960s. According to this system a small number of primary, secondary and higher-level schools selected on the basis of their general conditions and the past performances of their students at the university entrance examinations, receive priority as regards financial appropriations, equipment and the appointment of competent teachers, and they can choose the most promising students through competitive examinations. The system provides a network within which high-quality studies are secured, and sets a standard for the improvement of other schools.

In institutions of higher learning, the restoration of the seminar for teaching and research, (*jiaoyanshi,* the equivalent of the Soviet *kathedra,* a professional group directing and supervising professional work on one subject in a discipline), has been coupled with a new autonomy of each department (*xi*) as regards the practical organization of studies,

11

teaching assignments, division, length and content of courses. Moreover, increasing power is left to the universities concerning the curriculum and the definition of standards; and within universities, authority on such decisions belongs now to professionals rather than to political cadres. Although limited to academic subjects, intellectual freedom as understood in the 'let a hundred schools contend, let a hundred flowers blossom' slogan provides also access to a much wider range of knowledge and a development of critical analysis and innovation.

Last but not least, some real budgetary effort has been allowed. State expenditure for education has increased by some 8 to 9 per cent per year since 1978.[15] Although exact figures on the distribution are not available, it is known that a major part goes to higher and technical education which can also benefit from research contracts with industry or government agencies. The efficiency of this financial improvement should not, however, be overstated. More than three-quarters of the budgetary increase has been eaten up by a long-needed wage rise.[16] On what is left for developing educational facilities, misappropriations of funds do happen, as testified by the lately much-publicized case of Deqing district in Zhejiang Province where from 1979 to 1981 one-quarter of the budget earmarked for education was used to establish a foundry and build fashionable apartments for the educational bureau cadres.[17] Of wider weakening impact is the rate of inflation which has kept around 6 per cent until 1981.[18] Finally, while in most countries educational expenditure runs at between 10 and 30 per cent of public expenditure, remaining below 10 per cent only in a few countries such as Gambia, Jordan, Indonesia or the Philippines, China still spends only 9 per cent of her budget on education,[19] but 15 per cent on the military.

Looking at the qualitative aspect of the problem, Chinese perspectives for the training of highly-qualified personnel seem very promising indeed. A wide consensus exists on the necessity of carrying out such a programme, and a set of useful measures has been taken for this purpose. Foreign scientists generally agree also that the proportion of outstanding students seems now relatively higher in Chinese universities and colleges than in other countries. But the Chinese government plans make plain that the opportunity for such a training will be restricted to a very limited number.

*The Individual: Lack of Education, Employment, and
Opportunities for Upward Social Mobility*

On the second main issue - the need to insure professional
and social integration of all the younger generation -
public opinion and government policies also show dis-
crepancies. There is general awareness and open recognition of two related problems: unemployment and the moral
crisis among the youth. Government authorities admit the
existence of a large urban unemployment figure, rising to
30 million people.[20] Among them the proportion of
youngsters reaching job age in the current year amounts to
an average of 27.7 per cent, while most of the remainder
are young people as well, who have come of age in recent
years.[21] Official quarters have up to now taken for
granted that youth reaching job age in the rural areas all
found employment in agriculture and sideline activities:
these young people would indeed share in the distribution
of work-points in their village, whatever that means in
actual occupation and income. But with the recent general
spread of the household responsibility system for production and labour which stimulates productivity, the existence of underemployed and unemployed rural surplus labour
is likely to become more conspicuous and embarrassing in
the near future. Some high cadres have been quoted outside
China as admitting unofficially a figure of 100 million
unemployed. Whether this figure is a guess or a fact, the
generations now reaching job age number from 27 to 29
million each year, of whom about 6 million are graduates
from lower middle school and 6 million from higher middle
school. In the last three years the government has been
able to 'make arrangements' (*anzhi*) for only 8 million of
them every year, by providing in many cases some sort of
occupation rather than a real job.[22]
    Even if the public is aware of a more serious unemploy-
ment problem than the authorities wish to admit openly,
one affecting the countryside as well as the cities, and
especially with respect to school graduates, both sides
agree on the moral crisis affecting the youth. Increase
of youth delinquency has been abundantly featured in the
Chinese press since 1979, which is a new development.
But even more strikingly, the wide-spread loss of faith in
socialist ideology, the moral despair, scepticism or
cynical pursuit of selfish gain, have also been major
themes in literature dealing with or addressed to the youth.
Some foreign observers may have overstated the extent of
moral damage. Its assessment as found in an investigation
conducted by written questionnaires in 1980 among about a
thousand young people in factories, villages, schools and

urban quarters in Fujian and Anhui Province, and published
in the *Renmin Ribao* (People's Daily),[23] is probably an
optimistic estimate but shows nevertheless significant
critical and negative judgements and attitudes towards the
Communist Party's political and moral tenets. Among the
youngsters who answered, less than two-thirds were utterly
convinced of the superiority of the socialist system, and
only 53.4 per cent really believed that the four modernizations would be achieved before the end of the century.
Even though only 3.6 per cent confessed that they had no
ideal or had lost it, the ideal of barely one-tenth of them
was to struggle for the communist cause, and one-third only
expressed altruistic concerns in their rules of personal
behaviour. But for 70 per cent, the main social concern
related to the improvement of knowledge, science, technology
and skills.

To cope with the problem of professional and social
integration of the youth, two sets of remedies have been
clearly recommended and are now being applied: action on
educational structure and action directed at changing young
people's mind and behaviour.

Public attention has especially focused on structural
reform of the educational system. The wish has been widely
expressed that ordinary secondary schools be converted into
technical schools. Since the prospect for entering university looks slim in most cases, parents and teachers favour
the technical middle schools (*zhongdeng jishu xuexiao*), as
they existed before 1966, which gave children a training
that secured them a good position (mostly factory employment), and in which the job assignment was taken care of by
the State.

The government has repeatedly voiced its support of a
sounder balance in secondary education between general and
technical studies, but the policies it has engaged in, in
this respect, do not exactly meet real popular wishes.
Indeed some technical middle schools which had been closed
down during the Cultural Revolution reopened their doors
and some more have been created. The official figures are:[24]

year	number of schools	number of students
1965-1966	871	392,000
1979-1980	1,980	714,000
1980-1981	2,052	761,300
1981-1982	2,170	632,100

A recent drop in student enrolment can be noticed; it concerns only agricultural technical middle schools. It comes
partly from the recognition that many of those schools did

not have adequate standards, and partly from the fact that the recent loosening of government control over agricultural production and management makes it more difficult to find proper job assignments for the graduates.[25]

Ordinary secondary schools subjected to transformation are being turned essentially into vocational schools (*zhiye xuexiao*), not into technical schools. The important difference between the two is that, although the State may help to recruit specialized teachers and to provide necessary equipment, it neither takes the responsibility for them nor for the employment of graduates. The policy of converting a large number of ordinary middle schools into vocational schools is in fact a restoration of the double-track system as it existed in 1965 with the half-work half-study (*bangong bandu*) schools on one hand, and the regular university preparatory schools on the other. By the first half of 1982, an average of 6 per cent higher middle school students was engaged in such new programmes; the proportion reached 36 per cent in Liaoning Province.[26] Although the idea of running such programmes on a full-time basis has not been discarded, it seems that in many cases they may follow the principle of *qin gong jian xue* (hard work and thrifty studies) borrowed from the 1910s and early 1920s, which amounts to former half-work half-study. While these schools will not open the way to glory or to any really secure position,[27] the reform tends to sever the connection between secondary and higher education.

The same trend can be observed in another recent structural reform, namely the reduction in the number of key schools. After the restoration of these schools in 1977, there had been a tendency to increase their number so that it far exceeded the actual material means of the authorities upon whom they depended. Moreover, since the criterion for the recognition of a school as a key school was the number of its students who gained entrance to the university, the whole teaching focused on preparation for the examinations. The result was that the students who did not feel capacity or appeal for competition would lose interest or even drop out without anybody having cared to give them any real training: the system would then produce idle, sceptical, unmotivated youngsters. Of those who tried to the end, a high percentage would nevertheless not succeed in entering the university and would tend to become disappointed, bitter, unhappy and difficult to employ in other jobs. Furthermore, many firms and agencies do not care to get manpower of a high cultural level.

In the autumn of 1980 the number of key schools had thus been reduced. Only 700 at the secondary level now belong to what is called 'first-rank priority' (*shoupi zhongdian*).[28]

It seems that the system is heading for the establishment of an entrance quota for the university reserved for the best middle schools.[29] Such a device would just transfer the competition down to lower stages, at the entrance to junior then to senior middle school, and would make it even more difficult for graduates from ordinary district middle schools to fight their way up to higher education.

During the Cultural Revolution, the solution adopted to prevent the evil effects of a school system streamlined on the university entrance examinations had been to sever the link between success in school work and urban tertiary jobs: everybody after graduating from middle school was sent out to labour in the villages or factories, and promotion came later, on non-academic criteria. The present solution is to isolate the university channel. In first-rank priority schools senior middle education is now three years instead of two; primary education in first rank priority primary schools is six years instead of five. Through this institutional separation the authorities hope to cleanse and improve the whole educational system.

But action to promote professional and social integration of the youth is not limited to institutional reforms; it also includes ideological methods and tries to influence youth behaviour and mentality.

A large number of parents have shown concern at the loosening of basic moral and political instruction. In cities worries are expressed about 'contagion of Western vices' and above all about rising youth delinquency.[30] A trend in public opinion supported by a large number of the cadres favours the restoration of ethics and even some ideology.

In April 1980 the Ministry of Education and the Youth League called for a reinforcement of ideological work and political instruction. Several measures were adopted at the conference on education held in Tianjin in early December 1980. Following it, the political teaching staff was built up again: instructors were recruited and courses reorganized. Since autumn 1980 a course in Marxism-Leninism has become compulsory in higher education. In addition, students in natural sciences are required to take a course in Party history, one in political economy and one in philosophy, each of seventy hours at least. In the humanities, students must take, in addition, courses in the history of the international communist movement and in scientific socialism, each of at least 105 hours. In middle schools the programme of the early 1960s has been resumed. It is closely inspired by Soviet Union practice, and leads gradually from ethics for the youth to basic political knowledge of the constitution, to history of society and dialectical materialism.

Behaviour and moral attitudes have been included again among the criteria for admission to the university since 1981.

The most recent reform concerns the introduction of a curriculum for ideological and moral education in primary schools. Experiments have been conducted since autumn 1981, and a full text has been promulgated by the Ministry of Education in May 1982. The text has been widely publicized by a meeting held by the Department of Propaganda on 6 July 1982, where all concerned ministers and Party leaders gave speeches, and by numerous comments in the press.[31] The programme aims at educating 'a new generation who will have ideals, virtue, culture and discipline'. The content is supposed to be communist ideology. Its basic tenet is the 'five loves' (*wu ai*: love of country, people, labour, science and socialism), as it also was in moral education given in the 1950s. In fact the programme is mainly ethical and patriotic, very much in the line of what was taught in French primary schools in the early years of the Third Republic. The political content is diluted with morals of righteousness, effort, frugality, selflessness and scientism. Interestingly enough, children do not learn about Mao Zedong until the third year, but they will also have to wait until that time before they are encouraged to observe and ask questions.

Frequent intimidation campaigns against the independence of intellectuals and the abuses of cadres may serve as reminders that higher status does not guarantee safeguards. But for the time being the attempt to set directly on youths' motivations, as was tried during the Cultural Revolution, seems to have been dropped. The reason may be partly a determination to break away from the unhappy experience of that period, but it is more likely the fact that because job opportunities are inadequate, it is useless to tie up young people's expectations to any specific employment.

Official reform measures clearly echo a strong public demand for the improvement in the functional capacity of the educational system, in its ability to train people to find a niche in society and to contribute to the raising of its living conditions. But it is questionable whether these reforms actually meet public demand and whether they are conducive to a workable and acceptable organization of society.

THE BLUEPRINT FOR SOCIAL ORGANIZATION

Even if Chinese leaders have been pressed by necessity rather than determined by choice, the future society outlined by the educational reform measures of the last few years is indeed a partitioned society organized along a strict hierarchy.

Competition and ambition for promotion, which foreign observers have rightly pointed out as striking features in the new educational system, are reserved for urban youth who, because of more efficient birth-control in the cities, represent but a small fraction of the 20.6 per cent urban population. A recent public statement by the Vice-Minister and Party Secretary of the Ministry of Education, Zhang Chengxian, left no ambiguity about such a policy. He wrote that education in rural areas should be reformed in order to raise the level of the rural economy rather than to help people to leave the countryside and get promoted to the next school grade. Already by now only 20 to 30 per cent of rural junior middle school graduates enter senior middle school; and for rural areas the admission rate to the university is less than the 4-5 per cent national average, so that most students go back to production. For a rather long time to come, writes the Vice-Minister, rural school children will have to remain in the countryside and participate there in production. Only one full-time regular middle school will be kept for every 100,000 inhabitants, all other middle schools will become agricultural or vocational, eventually with the half-work half-study system.[32]

It should be noted also that the number of candidates for university entrance examinations has drastically decreased since 1978, falling from 6 million to 1.8 million in 1982, although the average number of senior middle school graduates exceeds 6 million every year.[33] In 1979, 53.33 per cent of the candidates to university entrance examinations came from rural areas.[34] In 1980, a preliminary examination eliminated 1.38 million candidates, leaving only 3.31 million for the decisive competition.[35] It seems that in the following years candidacy may have been further restricted to urban graduates.

With the new principles requiring that cadres should be recruited according to their level of education and technical ability,[36] political and social leadership is also reserved for those urban youths who may gain access to the best middle schools and to the university. Below this professional urban élite will lie the undifferentiated, subservient rural masses. Those masses will not be left ignorant but will receive only the limited training pertaining to their immediate livelihood in their local environment.

The Future Prospects of an Urban Technocracy

Is such a social blueprint a workable one? The question is
not only whether it can be made generally acceptable to the
Chinese citizens but also whether it can actually become
the pattern of social organization and social relations.

Let us remark firstly that as it now stands Chinese
society is already partitioned and organized along a strict
hierarchy. In terms of economic privileges, social prestige and power, and even in some aspects of civil rights,
cadres are obviously above commoners and apart from them.
Among the cadres themselves several groups can be identified
which do not permeate each other and which are each governed
by rigorous scales of privileges: local cadres, State cadres,
Party cadres - each has its rules and grades. In the same
way, commoners are divided into categories - peasants, work-
men, and employees, - which imply not only occupational
differences but a whole set of different rights and opportunities, further complicated by the interference of the
class-status (*jieji shenfen*)system left over from the early
1950s and not abolished even if some of its worst implications regarding the hereditary status of landlord have
been suppressed.

Such a divided hierarchical society is by now accepted or
at least endured by the Chinese people, so that there is
little ground to support the view that division and hierarchy are of themselves unacceptable to them. However, the
criteria of present-day partition and hierarchy in society
are not technical and scientific competence, as featured in
the social blueprint outlined by educational reforms. The
actual criteria are those of political commitment, of
ability to command, of connection to actual power, that is
to Party, State administration and army. It means that in
order to realize the new social blueprint, the values that
rule the present hierarchy must be changed. The substitution naturally meets with resistance from those who benefited from former criteria; they fear that their authority
might be challenged, that they may lose their position and
that their children may be feared to step down on the social
ladder. Such resistance has been forcefully exposed in the
Chinese press, in the speeches of Deng Xiaoping and his
close followers, and it certainly contributed to the bar-
gaining power of some army leaders at the recent Twelfth
Party Congress.

There is reason to believe, however, that resistance
from beneficiaries of the old system is not a major obstacle and can be successfully overcome. For one thing,
among the 19 million cadres, 63 per cent have attained the
level of senior middle school education or above, and 43 per

cent are specialists or technicians;[37] the latter would not
be hurt by the change which would affect at most only about
half of the cadres' membership. The substitution of new
hierarchical criteria certainly favours the intellectuals
who get the best chance for their own promotion, and whose
children enjoy at home an environment more conducive to
academic success than others. But at least by their economic means and urban residence, many cadre families are still
in a better position to have their children get the education
required for promotion than ordinary peasants and working-
class families. Moreover, the introduction of a new hierarchy is coupled with rejuvenation of responsible personnel,
so that by the help of retirement, which for most cadres did
not exist before, a gradual slipping away from a political
to a technical élite can be achieved. Such a move towards
technocracy was already in progress in the early 1960s and
was eventually stopped by the Cultural Revolution.

The real obstacles to the smooth enactment of the new
social blueprint could well rest on grounds other than the
resistance of beneficiaries of the old system: the con-
straints that the State system imposes on social mobility,
and the protest from those who are left out of official
promotion opportunities.

Even though Party leaders claim that criteria of technical competence are being adopted for cadres recruitment,
the power system remains based on political commitment and
Party monopoly, so that the very organization of power,
even more than the mentality of power-holders, is in fact
checking a true renewal of the ruling élite as regards
qualifications as well as social origins.

The Party may well sincerely look for technical performance to retrieve its shaking credit, but its specific role
and very existence depend on ideological and political
principles. It is unlikely (indeed formally ruled out by
current regulations) that somebody should be recruited as
a cadre on the basis of his diploma in finance if he is
known to reject socialism and Party authority. But even so,
or in the case when the qualified cadre has faked commitment
to Marxism-Leninism, his professional action is bound or
determined by bureaucratic rules and a whole administrative
framework that stem out of political ideology, such as the
enforcement of democratic centralism or centralized planifi-
cation. The actual impact of the professional criteria for
recruitment could then well be offset by the necessity for
the new élite to operate within political conformity before
technical requirements can really be considered. What
happened in the Republican period when graduates from modern
schools replaced officials selected through the traditional

examination system, but could hardly achieve more than the latter, may well be true again.

Gradual access of elements from lower layers of society to the ruling strata may also become almost impossible. While upward social mobility of individual families seems to have kept at a reasonable rate during Ming and high Qing times,[38] from the late nineteenth century on mobility grew so intense as to lead to instability. The establishment of the communist regime brought about the last wave of reversal in social situations, in the early 1950s. But since that time, social circumstances have been practically frozen: upward family mobility appears to have become rare and restricted by such rules and practices as the system of hereditary class-status, government assignment and management of manpower, and regulations on travel and residence. This lingering situation contributed to the early enthusiasm for the Cultural Revolution and its promise of social change. But hopes were deceived. It is doubtful that any significant change will be brought about in this respect by the current educational reforms which restrict competition for promotion to the urban youth, and which do not provide additional means for poor families to support their gifted children all the way up through the long regular school curriculum.

Youth from intellectual families (in the large sense, including teachers, medical workers, technicians and engineers), are indeed likely to find now more opportunities for upward mobility, but although their families had little or no share in political power, they did not remain at the bottom as regards actual social conditions. Children from industrial workers' background may be losers in a competition where academic culture receives more and more emphasis, while the former system put a premium on their origin once they had successfully passed through the first stages of the academic race. Youth from the rural areas are simply denied any channel of access to the new ruling élite. Although the support of a few regular ordinary rural middle schools may give to some very exceptional peasant children a possibility to ascend the official ladder, current policy statements fail to emphasize or even to mention the opportunity for upward mobility which in the past had been a basic tenet in propaganda, even though seldom apparent in practice.

That government rhetorics should now avoid illusory promises is not likely to stir up any popular resentment. But the ban on rural youth runs against the very legitimation of the Party's power as the party of the labouring people, peasants included. It also applies not only to peasants' children but to cadre children whose parents are assigned to work in the countryside, as well. Although they cannot be voiced publicly for the time being, fears and discontent

resulting from this situation provide a large potential
constituency for opposition factions in the top power contest.

Another difficulty in establishing the rule of a new type
of élite may come from the social consequences of recent
economic reforms in rural areas. Within one or two years,
the introduction of the household responsibility system for
production and management (*bao chan dao hu bao gan dao hu*),
now carried out in 74 per cent of the brigades,[39] has
quickly brought about important new social developments not
yet mentioned in Chinese media but testified to by Chinese
and foreign observers.[40] Since all profit, except a rather
small fixed share for the State, goes to each family, labour
becomes more intensive so that, the plots being small, some
members are often free to engage in activities that will
maximize profit. This has meant first going to the neighbouring market town to sell one's own products. But
commercial entrepreneurship is very rapidly expanding beyond
parochial limits. It involves marketing the production of a
few families or of one or several villages, getting commercial contracts from district firms and even distant cities
in every part of the country, providing supplies in certain
goods for business in the village, providing transport,
machinery or expertise. Through Chinese resourcefulness and
genius for using family and other connections, a whole informal network of commercialization and services is mush-
rooming nationwide. If this system is allowed to grow for
some time, which seems likely because the policy of concessions to individual peasant economy is necessary to Deng
Xiaoping's modernization programme, there will appear a
group of people who play an important role in social and
economic life without having been selected and legitimized
by State or Party authority.

Private management may be an outlet for the energies of
some youths, but it cannot really resorb unemployment because
it remains subjected to many limitations from State planning
and bureaucratic control.[41] The potential threat of social
or political protest by jobless or hopeless people will
therefore hardly recede. Moreover, the very existence of
such a group of successful managers will increase the
distance between the political apparatus or official élite
and society.

Conclusion

Let us now sum up the main points of the investigations and
draw some tentative conclusions.

The prospect is quite good for training a highly qualified élite among Chinese youth in restricted numbers.
Policies aimed at the professional and social integration
of young people at large may bring some improvement to the
present situation of widespread unemployment, lack of qualification, and feelings of frustration, scepticism or indifference. But they will not solve the basic problem of
opening enough jobs for the rising generations. Moreover,
these policies, as well as those designed to produce a new
élite, lead to a type of social organization and social
relations that is not likely to work out smoothly. The
ideological and political foundation of the power system and
its weight will make it difficult for the new élite to
assert its ability to innovate. Contrary to popular expectations, channels of upward mobility are not being expanded
and even get cut off for the numerous rural residents among
whom recent economic policies have allowed for an unfore-
seen accumulation of private wealth and for the rise of a
group of successful managers.

Does it mean that social crisis is ahead? It could be
argued from the findings of a recent book by Susan Shirk[42]
on career incentives in urban middle schools of the early
1960s, that competition based on academic criteria is less
divisive than when based on political criteria. Academic
competition applies standards that look fast, clear and objective; its judges stand outside and it is not mutually
destructive; it fosters acceptance by those who fail.
Therefore, to follow up this type of analysis, one could
view the future Chinese ruling élite as co-operating better
than the old one, less torn by fratricidal power struggles
and more nearly unanimously recognized by the people. But
such a wishful picture seems ruled out by the very small
number of available positions compared to the number of
candidates, and by the fact that rural youth are from the
start refused an opportunity to enter the race.

Open crisis, however, may not break out very soon, because the government avoids hard and fast measures as well
as a radical implementation of policies. Schooling is
being extended in order to slow down the arrival of young
people on the job market. Government support to agricultural mechanization has been dropped so that rural employment may not undergo a sudden decrease. Development of
labour-intensive light industry takes precedence over
capital-intensive heavy industry. University enrolment has
been slightly increased. Some additional access to and
recognition of higher education beyond the regular curriculum are provided through education by correspondence and
examinations for self-taught students. Such leeway may be
enough for some time to alleviate pressure in the cities,

especially since recent memories of the Cultural Revolution
provide a warning, effective in shaping public opinion
against violent confrontation. In the meantime, the new
economic policies in the countryside quell ambitions for the
pursuit of studies in the hope of obtaining official careers.
A prevailing new trend of indifference for academic achieve-
ments is noticed by many observers travelling to the
villages. And since the margin for operation and growth
depends entirely on the goodwill of the ruling Party and
State bureaucrats, the rising private managers are not in a
position to contest openly with the latter for political
power.

Adjustment, coexistence, resources and profit-sharing
between officials and social leaders, such as occurred in
imperial times, are more likely than direct challenge. But
one cannot help thinking how very vulnerable is this whole
balance of divided interests and of tightening and loosening
measures which shift back and forth from material incentives to moral indoctrination, or from technical pre-
requisites to political control. This balance is upheld by
Deng Xiaoping's personal skilfulness, authority and policies.
But if he should suffer a setback or simply disappear, the
deceived socially-ambitious citizenry could feed the ranks of
the opposition factions in the power competition, and
rampant social unrest could become an intractable issue
except by authoritarian measures and military means.

1. The school population figure is taken from the speech of the Vice-Minister of Education and the Party Secretary of the ministry, Zhang Chengxian, given to the Twelfth Party Congress, *Guangming Ribao*, 6 September 1982, p. 4. The youth population is only an approximation based on available estimates (see *Beijing Review*, no. 3, 16 January 1984, pp. 20-2), since data published from the national census conducted in July 1982 do not include as yet enough information about age structure. Such new information should have been the starting point of the present study which therefore must be considered only as a tentative assessment of issues.

2. The 1980 figure was given by *Beijing Review*, no. 13, 31 March 1980, p. 20. On the targets set in 1960 see 'La formation des cadres scientifiques et techniques en Republique populaire de Chine', *Notes et études documentaires*, (Paris, La Documentation francaise), no. 3576, 28 March 1969, p. 22.

3. *Zhongguo Baike Nianjian 1980*, p. 373. The report of Vice-Premier Fang Yi to the National Conference on Science is published in *Pékin Information*, no. 14, 10 April 1978, pp. 6-17.

4. *Zhongguo Baike Nianjian 1981*, p. 474.

5. *Guangming Ribao*, 11 July 1982, p. 1.

6. The revised draft of the plan has been published in *Guangming Ribao*, 13 December 1982, pp. 1-4.

7. *Zhongguo Baike Nianjian 1980*, p. 539. *Zhongguo Baike Nianjian 1981*, p. 471.

8. *Renmin Ribao*, 18 November 1982, p. 3.

9. *Guangming Ribao*, 15 August 1982, p. 1, and 29 August 1982, p. 3.

10. *Renmin Ribao*, 16 August 1982, p. 1.

11. *Zhongguo Baike Nianjian 1981*, p. 473.

12. *Guangming Ribao*, 1 November 1982, p. 1.

13. The enrolment announced for 1982 was 260,000: *Guangming Ribao*, 25 April 1982, p. 1.

14. *1982 Zhongguo Jingji Nianjian*, V, 391.

15. The last figure can be found in Finance Minister Wang Bingqian's report to the Standing Committee of the People's Congress, *Guangming Ribao*, 24 August 1982, p. 4.

16. *1982 Zhongguo Jingji Nianjian*, V, 388.

17. See *Guangming Ribao*, 26 August 1982, p. 1: 428,000 yuan are said to have been embezzled during the three years from 1979 to 1981. Several articles took up the issue in the following days.

18. Report by Wang Bingqian, *Guangming Ribao*, 24 August 1982, p. 4. He said that in 1981 this rate had been curbed down to 2.4 per cent.

19. *1982 Zhongguo Jingji Nianjian*, V, 320, 388. Until 1979 the rate remained between 5 and 6 per cent only: figures can be found in Qian Jiaju, 'Yao ba zengjia jiaoyu jingfei zuo wei shixian si hua de zhongyao zhanlüe cuoshi' (Increase of educational budget should be made an important strategic means of achieving the four modernizations), *Jiaoyu Yanjiu*, 1980, no. 2, pp. 6–11.

20. Feng Lanrui, Zhao Lükuan, 'Urban unemployment in China', *Social Sciences in China*, 1982, no. 1, pp. 131–2.

21. Ibid.

22. *Guangming Ribao*, 17 March 1982, p. 1.

23. Huang Zhijian, 'Jiujing yingdang ruhe renshi zhei yi dai qingnian?' (What should be thought of today's youth?), *Renmin Ribao*, 24 February 1981, p. 5.

24. *Zhongguo Baike Nianjian 1980*, pp. 535–6. *Zhongguo Baike Nianjian 1981*, p. 471. *1982 Zhongguo Jingji Nianjian*, V, 389.

25. See the thorough critique on the low quality of agricultural technical middle schools in Si Yi, 'Dui gaige nongcun jiaoyu de jidian kanfa' (Some views on the reform of rural education), *Guangming Ribao*, 20 December 1982, p. 2.

26. *Guangming Ribao,* 21 March 1982, p. 1. *1982 Zhongguo Jingji Nianjian,* V, 389. In Liaoning the proportion was raised to 41 per cent by the end of 1982: *Guangming Ribao,* 4 December 1982, p. 2.

27. See the straightforward comments in this respect in Si Yi's article quoted in note 25.

28. *Zhongguo Baike Nianjian 1981,* p. 476.

29. Stanley Rosen, 'Obstacles to educational reform in China', *Modern China,* Vol.8, No.1, January 1982, p.34.

30. Of the criminals caught between 1977 and 1980, 80 per cent were under the age of 25, while youths made up less than 20 per cent of criminal offenders before the Cultural Revolution; moreover, youths still in school made up 47 per cent of youth offenders: *Beijing Review,* 23 February 1981, p. 22.

31. The full text has been published in *Guangming Ribao,* 6 July 1982, p. 2. See also ibid., 8 July, p. 1; 9 July, p. 1; 10 July, p. 1; 28 July, p. 1.

32. Zhang Chengxian, 'Gaige nongcun jiaoyu wei jianshe shehuizhuyi xin nongcun fuwu' (Reform rural education to serve the building of the new socialist village), *Guangming Ribao,* 28 August 1982, p. 1. Also his speech quoted in note 1 above.

33. Figures for 1982 and 1981 in *Guangming Ribao,* 11 July 1982, p. 1. For other years, ibid., 26 December 1977, p. 2; 21 September 1979, p. 1; 4 July 1980, p. 1.

34. *Zhongguo Baike Nianjian 1980,* p. 538.

35. *Guangming Ribao,* 4 July 1980, p. 1.

36. For a record of important policy statements by top leaders and a detailed explanation on this issue, see the article by Song Renqiong, member of the new Political Bureau of the Central Committee, in *Renmin Ribao,* 2 October 1982, p. 2.

37. Ibid.

38. According to Ping-ti Ho, *The Ladder of Success in Imperial China,* the turnover of family membership in the ruling strata of officialdom reached one half in

each generation during Ming times and one third in Qing times.

39. *Renmin Ribao,* 22 August 1982, p. 1.

40. Since the Twelfth Party Congress, however, the Chinese press often publishes articles that praise individual peasants who become wealthy through their own enterprising spirit, and they provide illustrations of what I summarize below: e.g. *Guangming Ribao,* 13 November 1982, p. 1; ibid., 12 December 1982, p. 1; ibid., 10 December 1982, p. 1. In Qushan district, Anhui Province, an interesting case gives full evidence of rapidly-extending private business networks: the case received special publicity because the provincial party committee quashed the verdict of the district authorities who had condemned the young peasant businessman: *Renmin Ribao,* 6 January 1983, p. 2.

41. This is made clear by the arguments adduced in the decision of the Anhui party committee mentioned in note 40, which specifies all the delimiting rules which must not be infringed upon, and which had not been jeopardized by the business of the accused.

42. S. Shirk, *Competitive Comrades: Career incentives and student strategies in China.*

REFERENCES

Beijing Review. A Chinese Weekly of News and Views. Beijing.
Guangming Ribao (Brightness Daily). Beijing.
Ho Ping-ti 1982. *The Ladder of Success in Imperial China.* New York: Columbia University Press.
Jiaoyu Yanjiu (Educational Research), a monthly journal. Beijing.
Modern China. An International Quarterly of History and Social Science. SAGE Publications.
Notes et études documentaires. Paris, La Documentation francaise.
Pékin Information. A weekly magazine. Beijing.
Renmin Ribao (People's Daily). Beijing.
Shirk, Susan 1982. *Competitive Comrades: Career incentives and student strategies in China.* Berkeley, Los Angeles, London: University of California Press.

Social Sciences in China. *A Quarterly Journal*. Beijing.
Zhongguo Baike Nianjian (China Yearbook). Beijing.
Zhongguo Jingji Nianjian (Almanac of China's Economy).
        Beijing.

2

SOME PRELIMINARY NOTES ON CHINESE
JOKES AND CARTOONS

Christoph Harbsmeier

Editors' Introduction

*The ability to view one's own cultural and social predica-
ment with the smiling detachment of the joke is a hallmark
of civilization. China has a rich tradition of jokes and
these tell us something about how the Chinese react to
their own culture. Christoph Harbsmeier follows the history of Chinese jokes from their beginning in the classical
literature through various compilations of jokes from the
third century down to our time, with digressions into
Japanese and European jocular literature. In recent years,
the jokes in China seem to have been driven so far underground that many Chinese will deny that they exist any
longer. However, cartoons flourish in China today and the
author follows the history of Chinese cartoons with a few
examples of humorous paintings followed by a brief history
of cartoon periodicals in the 1920s and 1930s. The latter
half of the essay is an illustrated introduction to some
of the leading cartoonists in China today, such as Hua
Junwu, Liao Bingxiong, Ding Cong, and Fang Cheng.
Christoph Harbsmeier arranged exhibitions of his cartoon
collection at the Deichmann Library in Oslo, August 1982,
at the Royal Library in Copenhagen, December 1982, and at
Stanford University in May 1983.*

Every joke is a little revolution, said George Orwell. By
that token the Chinese have been a thoroughly revolutionary
people for a very long time. Consider the history of the
jest-book in traditional China. From the third-century
Xiaolin (Forest of Laughter) down to the nineteenth-
century *Xiaode hao* (Well Laughed) well over one hundred
jest-books have come down to us.

It would not be funny but ludicrous to pretend to
summarize such tremendous wealth of jocular folklore in a
few pages. However, one thing needs emphasizing: the rich
history of the Chinese joke provides sorely needed supplementary evidence on the *histoire de la mentalité chinoise,*
offering, as it does, an irreverent counterpoint to the
predominant public culture of traditional times. The jokes
poke fun at the very authorities who were unassailable in
real life. They deride the moralizing pomposity of public
life. They defy many of the taboos that seem so rigidly
enforced in traditional Chinese society.

For an understanding of the history of private conscious-
ness and sensitivity in China - as opposed to public Chinese
rhetoric - the jest books are invaluable sources. Jokes
tell you something about what it felt like to be a Chinese.
They tell you something about how the Chinese *react to* their
own culture. It is important to realize that civilized
people - past and present - are not just *representatives* of
a culture, they also *react to* their own culture. After all,
the ability to view one's own cultural and social predica-
ment with the smiling detachment of the joke is a hallmark
of civilization. Literary historians have neglected the
popular joke at their own peril.[1]

China's grand historian Sima Qian (145-*c*.76 BC), unlike
his modern successors, honoured the jesters by according
them a separate chapter of his *Shiji*. To the historian
Sima Qian the test of a good jester was not so much whether
he could tell a good joke but whether he could solve intractable political problems through the readiness of his wit.
Here is a sample of the effective use of sarcastic wit from
Shiji:

> Once the First Emperor made it known that he intended
> to set up a great game-reserve all the way from Box
> Valley Pass in the east to Granary Store in Yong in the
> west.
> 'What a marvellous idea!' said jester Twisty Pole.
> 'You could let loose a whole mass of wild beasts and
> birds in it. And then, if there's an invasion, you can
> just let the gazelles and deer butt them with their
> horns. That'll send them packing!'
> That was enough to make the First Emperor drop his
> scheme.[2]

CHINESE JEST-BOOKS

While historians were concerned with the political effec-
tiveness of jokes and wit, philosophers were often more
interested in their didactic use for moral enlightenment.
The book *Zhuang Zi* is notoriously rich in profound humour
and subtle jokes. The Han dynasty compilations *Shuo Yuan*
and *Xin Xu* turn up surprising bits of Confucian humour.
However, the first collection of jokes told for their
amusement value dates from the time of the 'free discussions' (*qingtan*) in the third and fourth centuries AD.
The *Xiaolin* (Forest of Laughter) of the third century AD,
of which about 50 pieces with various pedigrees of
authenticity survive today, is full of burlesque humour.
It predominantly represents the sort of sneering humour

which caused Plato and Aristotle to consider supercilious-
ness and disdainfulness to be constitutive elements of
humour.[3]

The next famous jest-book that has come down to us is
the *Qiyanlu* (The Book of Smiles), reputedly by a scholar of
legendary wit from the Sui dynasty, Hou Bo (*fl.* 581 AD). A
collection of 41 stories under his name survives in a
Dunhuang manuscript dated 723 AD, while 58 further pieces
survive in various other compilations. Judging from the
evidence we have Hou Bo must be regarded as a jester and a
trickster, a learned Till Eulenspiegel of the Far East.
Often Hou Bo uses his wit to solve political problems.
Occasionally he will tell a joke. But basically he must be
regarded as a man of the practical joke, the prank. Like
his somewhat more vulgar successor Xu Wenchang (1521-1593)
whose folklore continues to flourish to this day in Hong
Kong, Hou Bo soon became a legend. Many good stories of
varying origins have become attached to his name. Thus the
tricksters Hou Bo and Xu Wenchang suffered much the same
literary fate as their German cousin Till Eulenspiegel who
died in 1350 and whose exploits were first published in
Antwerp under the promising title *Ein kurtzweilig lesen von
Dyl Vlenspiegel.*[4]

In the People's Republic today, *Afanti* (i.e. the
legendary Effendi of the Turkish peoples) has taken over as
the most popular jester and trickster.[5] There have even
been made films of *Afanti*'s exploits in recent times, while
Hou Bo and Xu Wenchang have receded into the limbo of
arcane history.

The poet Su Dongpo (1036-1101) cultivated a very literary form of humour among his circle of friends. The
collection *Ai Zi zashuo* (Miscellaneous Sayings of Ai Zi)
consisting of 34 elegant literary pieces, is traditionally
attributed to Su Dongpo, but this attribution was already
doubted in Song times.[6]

The Ming dynasty scholar Lu Zhuo compiled a continu-
ation of the *Ai Zi zashuo* entitled *Ai Zi houyu* (Later
Sayings of Ai Zi) in 1576. In the introduction to this
collection Lu Zhuo writes: 'From my youth I have always had
a penchant for scurrilous tales. When I got hold of one I
invariably noted it down.'[7] The fifteen stories Lu Zhuo
noted down, like the original *Ai Zi zashuo,* are indeed
entertaining evidence of the humoristic sensitivity among
Song and Ming scholars.

The Ming dynasty was undoubtedly the golden age of the
Chinese jest-book. The folklorist and writer Feng Menglong
(1574-1646), justly famous for his marvellous collections
of short stories, also deserves great credit for collecting
and systematizing traditional Chinese jocular folklore.

His monumental *Xiaofu* (The Realm of Laughter) contains about 720 jokes. Most of these are traditional, but true to his habits in other areas of folklore Feng Menglong has taken the opportunity to compose quite a few new jokes himself. In his characteristically plain introduction to his collection Feng writes:

> The ancient as well as the modern world is one large realm of laughter. I myself and you my reader are within this realm, and we are both natural targets for gossip and ridicule. Without telling stories one does not become human. Without laughter one cannot tell stories. Without laughter and stories no world emerges. Oh Monk Budai! My master! My master![8]

It seems that Feng Menglong attempts to define man as a fabulating and a laughing animal. He clearly attaches metaphysical and/or religious significance to laughter and dedicates his book to the memory of an inspired humorous Buddhist monk Budai (died 917).

The *Xiaofu* is thematically organized with separate sections on officials, degenerate Confucians, paupers, doctors and magicians, priests, eccentrics, loafers and cripples. There is also an interesting section on everyday matters, and a rich collection of erotic jokes.

Not surprisingly, the *Xiaofu* became a resounding success. So much so that Feng was inspired to add two more collections: *Guang xiaofu* (The Realm of Laughter Enlarged), and *Gujintan'gai* (General Tales, Old and New).

Among the Qing dynasty collections of jokes Shi Chengjin's *Xiaode hao* (Well Laughed) is notorious for its persistent attempt to use the joke as an instrument of progressive social criticism. *Xiaode hao* has therefore become a happy hunting-ground for compilers of modern Chinese jest-books since 1949.

More popular than *Xiaode hao*, both in Qing times and afterwards, was Cheng Shijue's *Xiaolin guangji* (The Forest of Laughter Extended), a veritable gold-mine of traditional Chinese joculography.

On the other hand *Xiaolin guangji* did come in for some heavy criticism from the journalist writer Wu Jianren (1867-1910). Wu Jianren wrote a collection of jokes entitled *Xin xiaolin guangji* (New Forest of Laughter Extended), and in the preface he wrote:

> It is my humble opinion that among literary works serious prose is not as readily received as humorous talk. That is why collections of jokes are so well received. But Chinese joke collections are extremely stale. They all follow the same pattern and do not

33

give you any new insights or any new flavour. Among
these collections there is the *Xiaolin guangji* with
which even women and children are familiar. Regrettably
the contents of this collection are vulgar and undignified. They are all of them dirty jokes from the lower
strata of society. They bring their readers no gain.
On the contrary they are designed to provoke improper
desires. In order to improve on this situation I have
written the *Xin xiaolin guangji*.[9]

Traditionally, literary critics in China have indeed
taken a very dim view of jest books. Liu Xie (465-522)
points out disparagingly that *xie* 'humorous' is related to
jie 'all'. Jokes, Liu Xie complains, use shallow language
and are vulgar in conception.[10] Indeed, the earliest jokes
we have are all written in a mercifully plain and easy
style that contrasts sharply with Liu Xie's convoluted and
defiantly obscure prose.

Liu Xie finds it scandalous that the historian Sima Qian
should have condescended to devote a whole chapter of his
History to the jesters, and he hastens to explain that this
is because the jesters 'in spite of their extravagant one-
sidedness were ultimately aiming for righteousness and just
principles.'[11] Thus already Liu Xie explicitly declares
the conformist political purpose of the jesters as a
necessary excuse for accepting their humour. Cao Pei's
(188-227) practice of telling jokes for the fun of it is
disparaged by Liu Xie. And what makes things worse, in Liu's
eyes, is that 'hundreds of people have followed this path of
vulgarity.'[12]

Attitudes like Liu Xie's must have played their part in
preventing the transmission of most of the early Chinese
jokes. In a way it is quite surprising that so many jest-
books *have* survived in such a climate of élitist literary
taste.

The editors of the many modern selections of ancient
jokes invariably make it plain in their docile and innocent
introductions that jokes are important for their moral
(revolutionary) content, and not because they are simply
funny and enjoyable. But in their *selection* of ancient
jokes for reprinting, most modern editors, while studiously
avoiding all the erotic pieces, show an almost disconcerting
total tolerance for scatological detail. They most
certainly include many a good joke that cannot possibly have
recommended itself to them on ideological grounds.[13]

Here we have a modern phenomenon with a long and dis-
tinguished cultural history. Traditionally, the prefaces of
popular books very often provide the *excuse* for publication,
but not the real reason. The prefaces explaining that *Jin*

Ping Mei is a moralistic novel reinforcing the conventional notion of divine retribution are not very good evidence that this is how the novel was perceived by the writers of the prefaces, let alone by the reading public. The case of the modern jest-books is closely similar.

CHINESE, JAPANESE AND WESTERN JOCULOGRAPHY

Even the briefest survey of the Chinese joculographic tradition would be grossly incomplete without a note on the history of the Chinese jest-book in Japan. The Japanese, for all their sustained interest in graphic humour and caricature through the ages, first began to recognize the humorous story or joke as a proper form of literature during the Keicho period (1596-1614). During the seventeenth century 20 collections of Chinese jokes were published in the original Chinese. The golden age of the Chinese joke in Japan came during the Anei period (1771-1781). Within that glorious decade no less than 90 such collections were published, often with Japanese transliteration added to the Chinese characters.

The *Seisuisho* (Wake-Sleep-Laughter) published between 1624 and 1643 contains 990 jokes and counts as a model for the host of Japanese joke collections that were to follow. In any case it remained unsurpassed in size.

R.H. Blyth's eccentric *Oriental Humour* contains a rich and inspired anthology of Japanese jokes.[14] He rightly devotes a special section to the relation between Chinese and Japanese jokes.[15] The overall impression is clear enough. What the Japanese did was to refine and polish the Chinese jokes and to produce inspired jokes of their own that came to possess a very strong specifically Japanese flavour.

Working mostly from the Japanese, Blyth has also produced a brief anthology of Chinese jokes through the ages. More reliable translations are available in Giles 1925 and in Levy 1974 and 1964. The latter is to be particularly recommended for its bibliography.

I am painfully aware that this brief survey of Chinese joculography falls miserably short on examples. On this score I hope to make ample amends in another place, but let me insert at least one illustrated joke, *THE WORTHY NEO-CONFUCIAN* (see No. 1):

A worthy Neo-Confucian was walking along in his digni-
fied slow manner when it happened to start raining. The
man began to run for shelter. Then he developed a bad
conscience and said to himself: 'It is quite undignified
to run wildly. Now when a gentleman has made a mistake he
must not be afraid of making amends.' Then he braved the

rain again to return to where he had started to run and proceeded forward with well-measured steps.[16]

Before I turn to the graphic joke in China, a brief comparison with Western joculography is in place. The only collection of jokes that has come down to us from Greek and Latin antiquity is the *Philogelos* compiled around the fifth century AD,[17] and as far as I know this remained the only joke collection in Europe until the nineteenth or possibly eighteenth century.[18] Since the nineteenth century there has been an explosion of interest in jocular folklore in the West.[19]

In China there has been a rich flora of often Western-inspired joke collections from the 1920s onwards.[20] Lin Yutang played an important part in propagating literary forms of humour in journals like *Lunyu*.[21]

Since 1949, the political joke has been driven so far underground that many candid Chinese will deny that it exists any longer. On this point there is a striking contrast with the Soviet Union.[22] In the Chinese underground movements, on the other hand, it naturally plays an important part.

THE GRAPHIC JOKE IN TRADITIONAL CHINA

Consider now the history of the cartoon in traditional China. While the joke has been recognized as a literary genre in its own right since at least the third century AD the cartoon did not exist as an art genre until the end of the Qing dynasty.

This does not mean that there was no humour in traditional painting or that there were not certain isolated works that may plausibly be described as cartoons in traditional times. Bi Keguan and Li Chan[23] describe and reproduce fascinating examples of Chinese graphic humour dating from the fifteenth century onwards. Moreover, already during the thirteenth century the Buddhist painter Liang Kai came pretty close to cartooning when he portrayed the Zen patriarch tearing up a Zen-Buddhist sutra in his justly famous painting, *HUI NENG TEARING UP THE SUTRA* (see No. 2). Learned doubts concerning the authenticity of this painting need not concern us here.

The Ming painter Zhu Jianshen (1448-1477) has left us a unique work which must qualify as a profound literary cartoon, *SPIRITS UNITED* (see No. 3). It refers to a legendary visit by the poet Tao Yuanming (365-427) and the Confucian Lu Xiujing to the devoted Buddhist Hui Yuan (333-416). These three people of opposing philosophical convictions greatly enjoyed each other's company and quite thoughtlessly Hui Yuan violated his strict monastic rules of conduct by sending his friends off in the traditional way. When the three men discovered

this breach of monastic discipline they broke into laughter.
If one looks more closely at the cartoon one realizes that
what looks like one laughing person is in fact composed of
three faces. This is easily discovered by covering up one
half of the cartoon and looking at the rest. Zhu Jianshen's
cartoon celebrates the transcendent understanding symbolized
by laughter.

There clearly are humorous works among traditional Chinese
paintings. None the less, the contrast with Japan is
striking. The Japanese can look back on a millennium of advanced cartooning by many of their finest artists. Netto and
Wagener[24] reproduce and interpret over 250 humorous drawings
from Japan, and a similar book could never have been published on Chinese humour even with the much greater scholarly
resources at our disposal today.[25]

THE MODERN CHINESE CARTOON

As far as I know, the earliest set of ideological cartoons
were the broad-sheets directed against the missionaries.
Aleksejev 1966:145-153 and especially Garanin's fascinating
article from 1960 entitled *Kitajskij antikhristianskij lubok
XIX veka* (The Chinese anti-Christian cartoon in the nineteenth century) are standard works on this subject. The
style and technique of these anti-missionary works are
entirely traditional and closely similar to that of the New
Year pictures.

In China the strictly political cartoon first emerged in
places with a strong Western influence. Personal satire was
a Western-inspired innovation. A cartoon from the Tokyo-
based Chinese *Minbao* dated 25 April 1907 entitled *THE
TRANSFORMATION OF TRAITORS* depicts the politicians Zeng
Guofan, Zuo Zongtang and Li Hongzhang (see No. 4). The
cartoonist's personal attack on political opponents does not
have deep roots in China.[26]

The first specialized collection of cartoons was published
in 1916 by the *Shishibao* (Journal on Current Affairs) in
Shanghai as volume 20 of *Wushen quannian huabao* (Complete
Pictorial of the Year Wushen). The cartoon *STEALING BELLS*
from this collection satirizes the traitors who try to sell
out China without the Chinese people noticing (see No. 5).

The first collection of cartoons by an individual artist
was the *Guochi huapu* (A Picture Book of National Shame)
published in 1916 by Dan Duyu (1896-1972). (One recalls
that 9 May, 1915, the day when Yuan Shikai accepted the 21-
point treaty, was declared 'a day of national shame').
OPENING THE DOOR TO THE DEVIL is a representative cartoon that
attacks pro-Japanese traitors prostituting national dignity
(see No. 6).

Already in 1918 the first specialized journal of cartoons was published, the legendary *Shanghai Poke* (English subtitle: The Shanghai Puck). However, the Shanghai Puck remained a marginal phenomenon in the rich publishing world of Shanghai at the time.

In the wake of the May Fourth Movement the educational and propagandistic mobilizing potential of the cartoon as a mass medium was increasingly recognized. The humanist Feng Zikai (1898-1975) was the first artist to cultivate the cartoon as an independent lyrical art form which won wide acclaim in both artistic and literary circles. The modern Chinese word for cartoon *manhua* was first used for Feng's work (in 1924/5). Feng became the father of the artistic lyrical cartoon in China.[27]

However, Feng was in a way a political outsider, a Buddhist individualist. It was the task of his more politicized colleagues like Zhang Guangyu (1900-1965) and Lu Shaofei (born 1903) to transform the cartoon into an important satirical and propagandistic force. During the thirties there came a wave of cartooning periodicals with titles like *Shidai Manhua* (Modern Sketch), *Manhua Shenghuo* (Cartooning Life), *Pangguanzhe* (The Onlooker), *Zhongguo Manhua* (Chinese Cartoons), *Manhuajie* (The Cartooning World), *Shanghai Manhua* (Shanghai Cartoons). In all, there were at least 17 such cartooning periodicals.

By far the most important of these was *Shidai Manhua* of which 39 issues were published between 1934 and 1937. The more left-wing *Manhua Shenghuo* (Cartooning Life) was closed by the Guomindang government after only 4 issues, and some of the other periodicals were even more short-lived.[28] Although the cartooning periodicals of the thirties were predominantly 'progressive' in outlook and tended to oppose Guomindang repression, they were essentially commercial ventures. In order to attract a sufficient readership they did not shrink from sexy covers as well as lurid comic strips. Indeed, many art critics of the thirties and forties complained about the artistic shallowness and commercialized vulgarity of all too many cartoons.[29]

Another obvious way of attracting a permanent readership was the serialized comic strip (*lianhuan manhua*) which was introduced in the late twenties. Lu Shaofei (born 1903) created a Dr. Reform (*Gaige boshi*) who was intensely popular around 1929. Ye Qianyu (born 1907) introduced his Mr. Wang in 1928, and this figure remained hugely popular until 1937.[30]

Ye Qianyu stopped publishing comic strips in 1937. During the forties Zhang Leping's San Mao became the legendary hero of the comic strip scene. *San Mao liulangji* (An Account of San Mao's Wanderings) was a resounding success for many years. It was succeeded by the increasingly propagandistic

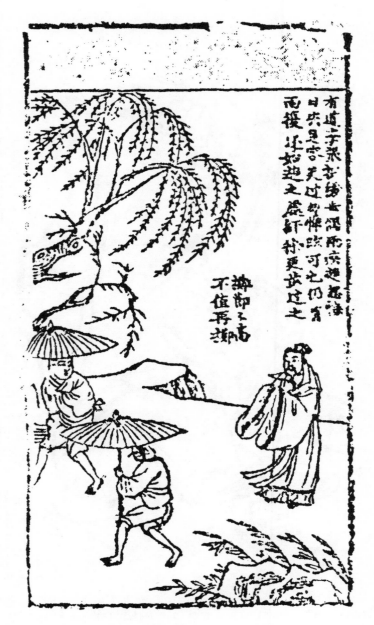

1. THE WORTHY NEO-CONFUCIAN

2. **HUI NENG TEARING UP THE SUTRA**, by Liang Kai (13th cent. AD)

一团和气
明·朱见深（成化皇帝）画

3. SPIRITS UNITED, by Zhu Jianshen (15th cent. AD)

过去之汉奸变相图（指曾国藩、左宗棠、李鸿章）

4. THE TRANSFORMATION OF TRAITORS, Anonymous (1907)

5. **STEALING BELLS**, Anonymous (1916)

6. **OPENING THE DOOR TO THE DEVIL,** by Dan Duyu (1916)

7. SAN MAO PAST AND PRESENT, by Zhang Leping (1979)

8. THE POLITICAL WEATHERCOCK, by Hua Junwu (1957, redrawn 1980)

9. EXTREME SUSPICION, by Hua Junwu (1980)

皇帝的新衣

10. THE EMPEROR'S NEW CLOTHES, by Hua Junwu (1980)

11. CAO XUEQIN HAS SOME OBJECTIONS, by Hua Junwu (1980)
'Why do you count how many white hairs I have got?'

病梅

12. A SICK PLUM TREE, by Hua Junwu

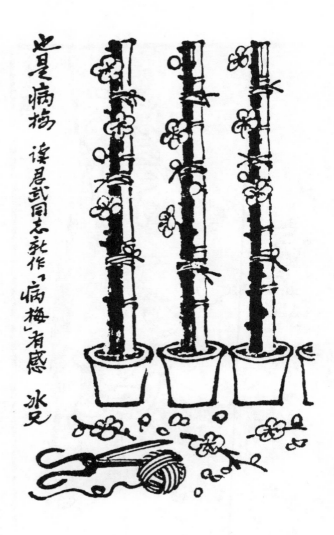

13. ANOTHER SICK PLUM TREE — A COMMENT ON HUA JUNWU'S
CARTOON, by Liao Bingxiong

也是武松?

14. ALSO A WU SONG?, by Mi Gu (1948)

15. ALSO A WU SONG?, by Liao Bingxiong (1981)

16a. IN 1907, AGED SEVEN, I WAS LEARNING BY HEART (see 16b)

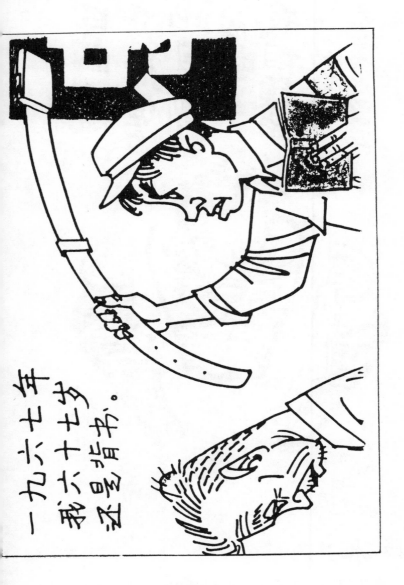

一九六七年
我六十七岁
还夏指书。

16b. IN 1967, AGED 67, I WAS STILL LEARNING BY HEART, by Liao Bingxiong (1980)

廖冰兄

17. AFTER THE TOPPLING OF THE FOUR EVILS, I HAVE DRAWN
THIS IN SELF-CRITICISM AND IN CRITICISM OF THOSE WHO ARE
LIKE MYSELF, by Liao Bingxiong (1980)

余悸病患者的噩梦

18. PORTRAIT OF SOMEONE RIDDEN BY A NIGHTMARE OF LINGERING
FEAR, by Ding Cong (1979)

武松打？

19. WU SONG STRIKING OUT?, by Ding Cong (1979)

20. PORTRAIT PRESENTED TO DING CONG, by Fang Cheng (1982)

教育

21. EDUCATION, by Fang Cheng (1980)

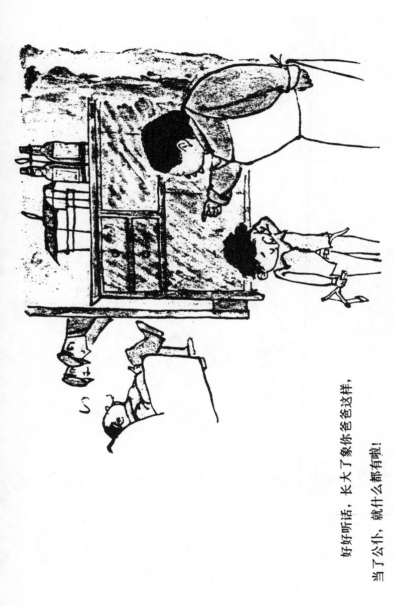

好好听话，长大了象你爸爸这样，

当了公仆，就什么都有啦！

22. 'NOW YOU LISTEN TO ME: IF YOU DO AS YOU ARE TOLD YOU WILL BECOME A PUBLIC SERVANT LIKE YOUR FATHER AND YOU'LL BE JUST FINE!', by Fang Cheng (1980)

文艺创作

23. ARTISTIC CREATIVITY, by Fang Cheng (1980)

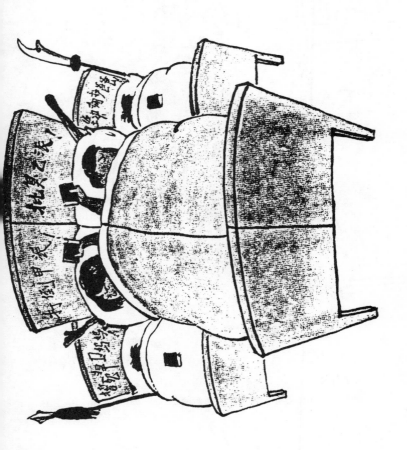

24. 'LET US TAKE THE CLASS STRUGGLE INTO THE FAMILIES!',
by Fang Cheng (1980)

武大郎开店

——我们掌柜的有个脾气，比他高的都不用。

25. A BIT OF A DWARF, by Fang Cheng (1980)

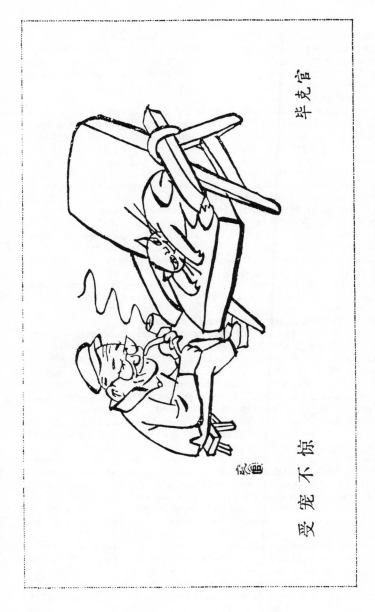

受 宠 不 惊

毕克官

26. TOO LOVED TO BE DISTURBED, by Bi Keguan

San Mao congjunji (San Mao Follows the Army), *San Mao ying
jiefang* (San Mao Welcomes Liberation), and in most recent
times by *San Mao xue kexue* (San Mao Studies Science). Zhang
Leping's cartoons after 1949 retain little of the freshness
and the humour that made him famous in the forties. See
SAN MAO PAST AND PRESENT (No. 7).

The 1930s were undoubtedly the crucial years in the formation of the modern Chinese cartoon. Of the grand old men,
Feng Zikai and Zhang Guangyu are no longer alive, but the
third grand cartooning man of the thirties Ye Qianyu is today head of the Academy of Fine Arts in Beijing and continues to inspire the younger generation. The leading
active cartoonists today all belong to the generation that
made their debut during the thirties: Hua Junwu, Fang Cheng,
Ding Cong, Liao Bingxiong, Jiang Yousheng, Zhang Ding,
Zhang Wenyuan, Wang Yisheng, Shen Tongheng. All these
leading cartoonists learned their trade during the thirties,
became increasingly politicized in the late thirties and
forties and have worked with Chinese newspapers and magazines since 1949.

The main division was between those who joined the communist propaganda teams in the liberated areas at an early
stage and those who fought the battle for a New China within
the area dominated by Guomindang forces. The former have
tended to become political cadres responsible for the arts,
the latter have tended to remain in positions of lesser
administrative and ideological responsibility. Each of
these two courses of action involved its own burdens and
opportunities for the artists concerned.

Take the case of China's most publicized cartoonist today,
Hua Junwu. He speaks with the polished, quiet authority of a
high official, and that is indeed what he is: one of the most
powerful figures on the Chinese artistic scene. As a member
of the Communist Party since 1940, vice-president of the
Chinese Artists Association in charge of daily administration
you would have thought that he must be an apparatchik and a
conformist. But one cannot fail to notice the naughty glint
in his eye and the smooth irony lurking underneath his
speech. In fact, Hua Junwu is the sharpest and the most
cerebral satirist of that very hierarchy in which he holds an
elevated position. One might call him the state jester at
the communist court. Being at the court he has the courage
to articulate what others quietly think, and being so close
to the centre he knows how far he can go.

Of all modern Chinese cartoonists, Hua Junwu is by far the
most popular. Certainly *not* because he is a spokesman of the
party. Moreover, since he draws often provocatively clumsy
and ugly pictures, it cannot be the graphic beauty of his
work that makes him so popular, either.

Hua Junwu likes to insist that he is an amateur. His mother told him to study mathematics, he reminisces with a smile, and one has little doubt he has the analytical intelligence to become a mathematician. But like many mathematicians he has an indomitable sense for buffoonery and the grotesque.

Since 1930, he says, he submitted cartoons in the tradition of nonsense-humour to various journals. And if one has not seen much of his early work in those journals, he submits, the reason is simple: almost all of his cartoons were rejected!

From 1934, however, he got his breakthrough in Lin Yutang's humoristic journal *Lunyu*, in *Shidai Manhua* and in *Shanghai Manhua*. Today, Hua takes a dim view of many of these early efforts.

Between 1938 and 1945 Hua worked for the communists at the Lu Xun Academy in the liberated Yan'an area. His cartoons from that period were either used as propaganda posters or they were published in the Party paper *Jiefang Ribao*.

In 1941 he organized a cartoon show in the liberated area, and in the summer of that year he was called up to Mao Zedong and told to dampen his satirical fervour. And would he make sure he was enjoined, that his satire was not understood to apply to the *whole* situation in Yan'an.[31]

From 1945 to 1949 Hua worked in *Dongbei Ribao* and drew mostly cartoons attacking American support for Chiang Kaishek. From 1949 he was employed as a journalist and cartoonist on the *People's Daily*, and he became already then an official in the Chinese Artists Association. Hua in 1954 gives an interesting survey of his production. Very little of his work from that period is of lasting value.

In 1957 Hua came forward with some of the most daring pieces of socialist self-criticism of the time, among which THE POLITICAL WEATHERCOCK (see No. 8). In 1958 he apparently had to make amends with a collection of anti-rightist cartoons.[32]

Hua's artistic breakthrough came in the mellower climate between 1959 and 1962. His collection of social cartoons from 1963 shows him at the height of his satirical powers.

Hua continued as editor in chief of the literature and art section of the *People's Daily* until 1966, disappeared - like most of his colleagues - and re-emerged in 1977 as the director of the Research Institute for Literature and Art under the Ministry of Culture, a position which he still holds today. His current satirical work seems to me to be every bit as lively and biting as anything he has done before the Cultural Revolution. In his cartoon EXTREME SUSPICION, for instance (see No. 9), could that little girl

be satirizing her cadre-father? *THE EMPEROR'S NEW CLOTHES*
(see No. 10), shows the literary sycophants imbued with blind
adulation. The subject of their absurd flattery is in fact
full of flaws and faults. This cartoon applies naturally
also to Western subservient literary criticism on modern
writers. Finally, in No. 11, *CAO XUEQIN HAS SOME OBJECTIONS*,
note the Westernized glasses of the mindless academic busy-
body - and his thoughtful wrinkles. Anyone who knows Hua
Junwu will suspect that this is *not* a cartoon on *Hongloumeng*
scholarship. (Cao Xueqin, born 1763 or 1764, author of the
novel *Hongloumeng,* A Dream of Red Mansions.)

Very occasionally, Hua Junwu drifts off into somewhat
schoolmasterly socialist didacticism, as in his cartoon *A
SICK PLUM-TREE* (see No. 12). This cartoon provoked an acid
response from the fearless old cartoonist Liao Bingxiong:
ANOTHER SICK PLUM-TREE - A COMMENT ON HUA JUNWU'S CARTOON
(see No. 13). In his original cartoon Hua Junwu had
criticized both crippling censorship under the slogan 'Things
must not grow' (written on the flower-pots in the upper half
of the cartoon), and unbridled wild cultural growth under the
slogan 'Trees must not be pruned' (on the trunk of the tree
below). Liao Bingxiong points out wrily that there is a
third and perhaps even more relevant danger in China today:
over-enthusiastic guided orthodoxy brought about by grotesque
ideological over-gardening.

Liao Bingxiong (born 1915) is perhaps the most controversial and irascible cartoonist today. Like his colleague
Hua Junwu he is concerned not with artistic virtuosity but
with the explosiveness of the message in his cartoons. Liao
Bingxiong is indeed a very explosive person to meet: fiery
in his enthusiasm and ferocious in his hostility towards what
he regards as the feudalist authoritarian mentality pervasive
in Chinese society. In 1948 the cartoonist and woodcut-
artist Mi Gu had attacked a cosmetic propaganda drive against
corruption in a most memorable cartoon, *ALSO A WU SONG?* (see
No. 14).[33] In 1981 Liao Bingxiong produced an up-dated
version of this cartoon attacking cosmetic anti-leftist
campaigns which caused considerable controversy, *ALSO A WU
SONG?* (see No. 15).

*IN 1907, AGED SEVEN, I WAS LEARNING BY HEART. IN 1967,
AGED 67, I WAS STILL LEARNING BY HEART* (see No. 16, a-b), is
a moving comment on the continuities of Chinese intellectual
history; and if you wonder what Liao Bingxiong feels like in
1980, there is a more up-dated self-portrait: *AFTER THE
TOPPLING OF THE FOUR EVILS I HAVE DRAWN THIS IN SELF-
CRITICISM AND IN CRITICISM OF THOSE WHO ARE LIKE MYSELF* (see
No. 17).

Compare the more Westernized self-portrait by another
grand old man of Chinese cartooning, Ding Cong (born 1916),

PORTRAIT OF SOMEONE RIDDEN BY A NIGHTMARE OF LINGERING FEAR, from 1979 (see No. 18). Fortunately, Ding Cong does not in the least strike one as a nightmare-ridden person when one meets him: he is a cheerful, jovial round man with a boisterous and infectious sense of humour. His tiny flat near Beijing University is so full of Western and Chinese art books that there is hardly room for him let alone a visitor. Ding Cong is probably the closest to a professional cartoonist you can find in China today. He also works as a graphic designer, and this shows in the graphic quality in his cartoons. A very fine series of them may be found in the literary journal *Dushu* (Reading Books) which regularly carries his work. *WU SONG STRIKING OUT?* (see No. 19) is Ding Cong's subtle satire on the contrast between propaganda and fact.

Fang Cheng (born 1918), the chief political cartoonist and journalist with *Renmin Ribao* since 1949, has produced a warm portrait of Ding Cong, *PORTRAIT PRESENTED TO DING CONG,* 1982 (see No. 20). Fang Cheng is a very mild and affable man. He is an artist at heart, an aesthete, technically brilliant and thoroughly familiar with traditional brush techniques, constantly learning from his artist friends. His home is full of marvellous Chinese brush paintings, his own exercises and other artists' presents. Until recently, Fang Cheng has published mainly international political cartoons as required by his paper, the *People's Daily*. Since 1979, he has come forward with remarkable fresh humoristic cartoons that have been exhibited with great success throughout China. Currently, Fang Cheng is writing a monograph on the concept of humour, and although he is well versed in Chinese tradition he has taken a considerable interest in Western things. A lavish two-tome edition of Wilhelm Busch's collected works in German holds pride of place in his study.

Having begun this very sketchy and impressionistic survey of Chinese cartooning with Liang Kai it is only natural to end with a florilegium of the gentle and profound cartoons by Fang Cheng.

Let us begin with *EDUCATION*, a self-portrait by Fang Cheng (see No. 21). Another comment on the realities of socialist education is No. 22, *'NOW YOU LISTEN TO ME: IF YOU DO AS YOU ARE TOLD YOU WILL BECOME A PUBLIC SERVANT LIKE YOUR FATHER AND YOU'LL BE JUST FINE!.'* In the next cartoon, *ARTISTIC CREATIVITY,* No. 23, the musician is reproducing the enthusiastic posture of the revolutionary on his score of musical notes. The inspired and more daringly original painter adds a shovel in a flourish of the impressionistic revolutionary imagination. The creative writer, out of respect for the correctness of the revolutionary stance, produces a poem in the shape of his model. The two figures in the background are

also deeply immersed in true revolutionary creativity. In
'*LET US TAKE THE CLASS STRUGGLE INTO THE FAMILIES*!' (see No.
24), the aims of the members of the family are stated over
their heads. In their dreams, the mother and father are
thinking: 'We must fight the X-Faction' and 'We must fight
the Y-Faction', respectively. The firm resolve of the child
next to the mother is: 'I solemnly swear to support my
mother', while that of the child next to the father is: 'I
resolutely support my father'. The parents have sticks with
which to beat the class enemy within the family, should the
need arise. In their sleep they uphold orthodoxy by holding
up orthodox books. Finally, No. 25, *A BIT OF A DWARF*, is
accompanied by the following explanation, offered to the
customer by the small waiter: 'You see, our master is a bit
of a dwarf. After retiring from his career as a peasant
revolutionary he opened this teashop, but he refused to
employ anyone who surpassed him'. An inscription in the
background says: 'The important thing for man is not to be
tall, it is to be powerful'.

I have briefly introduced a few of the most prominent
Chinese cartoonists of the older generation. Fortunately,
there are some fine younger artists who have developed their
own styles, men like Bi Keguan from Beijing, Yu Huali from
Tianjin and Zhan Tongxuan from Shanghai. I cannot help
seeing in these younger artists the torch-bearers of the old
Chinese jesting tradition. They are in any case truly heart-
warming people to meet. The last work to be presented here
is a conciliatory cartoon, *TOO LOVED TO BE DISTURBED* (No. 26)
by the leading historian of Chinese cartoons, Bi Keguan,
whose friendship and advice has sustained me in my all too
desultory excursions into the realm of Chinese humour.

1. Cf. Kao 1946 and Wells 1971 for interesting surveys of humour in traditional Chinese literature and art.

2. Cf. Dolby 1974, 177.

3. In *Laws* 816c Plato argues that although laughter leads to pride and vulgarity, the comic may be justified as a foil of the serious. Cf. also Plato's *Philebus* 48c ff. and Aristotle's *Poetics* 1449a.

4. For the role of the jester in Europe cf. Lefebvre 1968 and Deufert 1975, both of which contain outstanding bibliographies on mediaeval jocular subcultures.

5. Cf. the fascinating monograph Spies 1928.

6. Cf. Wang Liqi 1981, 70. Wang Liqi 1981 must be regarded as the standard reference work on Chinese traditional joculography and is the source for most other collections of jokes published in the People's Republic of China.

7. Ibid. p. 151.

8. Ibid. p. 300.

9. Cf. Wu Jianren 1981, 109.

10. Cf. *Wenxindiaolong, Sibubeiyao* ed. vol. 3, p. 18a.

11. Cf. Wang Liqi 1981.

12. Ibid.

13. Cf. Yan Hengbao 1980.

14. Cf. Blyth 1968, 199-564.

15. Ibid. p. 213-27.

16. Cf. *Jiuchou yezi*, published during the Wanli period 1574-1619, apud Wang Liqi 1981, 15.

17. The best text-critical edition of this outstanding collection is Thierfelder 1968. I hope to publish a detailed comparison between the *Xiaolin* and the roughly contemporary *Philogelos* in the near future.

18. For a brilliant survey of carnivalistic and humoristic subcultures of other kinds see Bakhtin 1968, 59-144.

19. Cf. the tightly printed bibliography in Röhrich 1980, 301-30.

20. Cf. Xu Zhuodai, no date, Zhang Genfa, no date, Anonymous (a), and Chen Xiaomei 1937.

21. Cf. Lin Yutang 1937.

22. For the history of graphic humour in the Soviet Union cf. Stykalin and Kremenskaja 1963. The published cartoons clearly bear no relation to the rich subversive folklore of the Russian joke.

23. Cf. Bi Keguan 1981, 8ff, Bi Keguan 1982, 1ff, and Li Chan 1978.

24. Netto and Wagener 1901.

25. Cf. Blyth 1968, chapter 17, and Wells 1971, 86ff.

26. Cf. Ye Qianyu 1982.

27. Cf. Harbsmeier 1983.

28. Cf. Bi Keguan 1982, 65.

29. Cf. Chen Wangdao 1935, 146 *et passim*. Erling 1978, 23 reproduces an extreme example where *Shidai Manhua* displays two bulging naked women on its cover.

30. Cf. Ye Qianyu 1981 for a rich selection of comic strips and contemporary cartoons.

31. Cf. Ai Zhongxin 1981.

32. Cf. Hua 1958.

33. Wu Song became a popular hero in the novel *Shuihuzhuan* because he slayed a dreadful tiger tyrannizing the people.

Ai Zhongxin 艾中信 1981. 'Hua Junwu bixia de manhua xingxiang' 华君武笔下的漫画形象 , in *Meishuyanjiu*, Beijing, 1981, no. 4, pp. 3-15.

Aleksejev, V.M. 1966. *Kitajskaja narodnaja kartina*, Moscow.

Anonymous, no date. *Hahaxiao* 哈哈笑 , Beijing: Renminwenxuechubanshe reprint.

Anonymous (a), no date. *Huaji duanpian xin xiaolin yiqianzhong* 滑稽短篇新笑林一千种 , Renminwenxuechubanshe reprint (original from the 1930s).

Anonymous, no date. *Xiaohua xintan* 笑话新谈 , Beijing: Renminwenxuechubanshe reprint.

Bakhtin, M. 1968. *Rabelais and His World*, Cambridge Mass.

Bi Keguan 毕克官 1980. 'Zhongguo manhua shi' 中国漫画史 , in *Yule Yuekan* 愉乐月刊 , Hangzhou, 1980, no. 4, 5, 6, 7, 8.

Bi Keguan 1981. *Manhua shitan* 漫画十谈 , Shanghai.

Bi Keguan 1981a. *Bi Keguan manhuaxuan* 毕克官漫画选 , Tianjin.

Bi Keguan 1982. *Zhongguo manhua shihua* 中国漫画史话 , Jinan.

Chen Puqing 陈蒲清 et al., ed. 1981. *Zhongguo gudai yuyanxuan* 中国古代寓言选 , Changsha.

Chen Wangdao 陈望道 1935. *Xiaopinwen he manhua* 小品文和漫画, Shanghai.

Cheng Shijue 程世爵 1899. *Yi jian haha xiao* 一见哈哈笑, Shanghai.

Ding Cong 丁聪 1981. *Ding Cong manhuaxuan* 丁聪漫画选, Tianjin.

Dolby, W. and Scott, J. tr. 1974. *War Lords and Other Biographical Sketches from a Chinese Prose Classic,* Edinburgh.

Eichhorn, W. 1940. 'Die älteste Sammlung chinesischer Witze. Eine Studie zur Literatur- und Kulturgeschichte des 2ten und 3ten Jahrhunderts', *Zeitschrift der deutschen morgenländischen Gesellschaft,* vol. 94, pp. 34-58.

Erling, J. and von Graeve, D. 1978. *Tigermaske und Knochengespenst. Die neue chinesische Karikatur,* Köln.

Fang Cheng 方成 and Zhong Ling 钟灵 1952. *Fang Cheng, Zhong Ling manhuaxuan* 方成钟灵漫画选, Beijing,1952.

Fang Cheng 方成 1956. *Manhua changshi* 漫画常识, Beijing.

Fang Cheng 1981. *Fang Cheng manhuaxuan* 方成漫画选, Tianjin.

Fang Cheng 1982. *Fang Cheng manhuaxuan* 方成漫画选, Shanghai.

Garanin, I.P. 1960. 'Kitajskij antikhristianskij lubok XIX veka', in *Ezhegodnik Muzeja istorii religiii i ateisma,* vol. 4, pp. 403-426, Moscow.

Harbsmeier, C. 1983. *The Cartoonist Feng Zikai (1898-1975),* Oslo.

Harbsmeier, C. (forthcoming). *Modern Chinese Image Literature,* London.

Hua Junwu 华君武 1947/8. *Rishi manhua* 日事漫画, Dongbeishudian.

Hua Junwu 1954. *Hua Junwu zhengzhi fengcihua* 华君武政治讽刺画, Beijing.

Hua Junwu 1958. *Hua Junwu manhuaxuan* 华君武漫画选, Beijing.

Hua Junwu 1962. *Wo zenmeyang xiang he zenmeyang hua manhua* 我怎样想和怎样画漫画, Shanghai.

Hua Junwu 1963. *Hua Junwu manhua xuanji* 华君武漫画选集, Beijing.

Hua Junwu 1980. *Hua Junwu manhuaxuan* 华君武漫画选, Beijing.

Hua Junwu 1980a. *Hua Junwu manhuaxuan* 华君武漫画选, Shanghai.

Hua Junwu 1981. *Hua Junwu manhua* 华君武漫画, Chengdu.

Hua Junwu 1981a. 'Manhua zasui' 漫画杂碎, in *Meishuyanjiu*, Beijing, 1981, no. 4.

Jenner, W. tr. 1982. *Satirical Cartoons from China*, Beijing.

Jiang Fan 江凡 1981. *Jiang Fan manhuaxuan* 江凡漫画选, Tianjin.

Jiang Yousheng 江有生 1981. *Jiang Yousheng manhuaxuan* 江有生漫画选, Tianjin.

Kao, G. 1946. *Chinese Wit and Humour*, New York.

Knechtges, D. 1971. 'Wit, Humour, and Satire in Early Chinese Literature (to AD 220)', *Monumenta Serica*, vol. 29, pp. 79-98.

Lefebvre, J. 1968. *Les fols et la folie. Etudes sur les genres du comique et la creation litteraire en Allemagne pendant la Renaissance*, Paris.

Levy, H.S. 1964. *Chinese Sex Jokes in Traditional Times*, Taibei.

Levy, H.S. 1974. *China's Dirtiest Trickster. Folklore about Hsü Wen-ch'ang*, Arlington, Virginia.

Li Chan 1978. *Zhongguo manhua shi* 中国漫画史, Shixichubanshe, Taibei.

Lou Tsek'uang 娄子匡 1970. *Songren xiaohua* 宋人笑话, The Chinese Association for Folklore, The Oriental Books Series, vol. 6, Taibei.

Miao Yintang 缪印堂 1981. *Miao Yintang manhuaxuan* 缪印堂漫画选, Tianjin.

Netto, C. and Wagener, G. 1901. *Japanischer Humor,* Leipzig.

Röhrich, L. 1980. *Der Witz, Seine Formen und Funktionen in Wort und Bild,* München.

Spies, O. 1928. *Hodscha Nasreddin. Ein türkischer Till Eulenspiegel,* Leipzig.

Stykalin, S. and Kremenskaja, I. 1963. *Sovetskaja satiricheskaja pechat',* Moscow.

Thierfelder, A. ed. 1968. *Philogelos,* München.

Wang Letian 王乐天 1981. *Wang Letian manhuaxuan*

王乐天漫画选, Tianjin.

Wang Liqi 王利器 ed. 1981. *Lidai xiaohuaji* 历代笑话集, Shanghai.

Wells, H.W. 1971. *Traditional Chinese Humour. A Study in Art and Literature,* Bloomington, Indiana.

Wu Jianren 吴茧人 1981. *Qiaopihua* 俏皮话, Guangzhou.

Xu Zhuodai 徐卓吊 ed., no date. *Xiaohua sanqian* 笑话三千,

Beijing: Renminwenxuechubanshe reprint.

Yan Hengbao 阎恒宝 ed. 1980. *Lidai xiaohuaxuan* 历代笑话选,

Taiyuan.

Yang Ruquan 杨汝泉 ed. 1933. *Huajishiwenji* 滑稽诗文集,

Hongkong.

Ye Qianyu 叶浅予 1981. *Cong sanshi niandai dao sishi niandai - Ye Qianyu manhuaxuan* 从三十年代到四十年代——叶浅予漫画选, Shanghai.

Ye Qianyu 1982. See Bi Keguan 1982, pp. 1-4, Preface.

Ying Tao 英韬 1981. *Ying Tao manhuaxuan* 英韬漫画选, Tianjin.

Yu Liang 俞良 1973. *Xu Wenchang quanji* 徐文长全集,
   Hongkong.

Zhang Genfa 张根法 ed., no date. *Youmo xiaohuaji* 幽默笑话集,
   Beijing: Renminwenxuechubanshe reprint.

Zhang Leping 张乐平 1963. *San Mao liulangji xuanji*
   三毛流浪记选集, Shanghai.

Zhang Leping 1978. *Erwazi* 二娃子, Shanghai.

Zhang Leping 1979. *San Mao ying jiefang* 三毛迎解放,
   Shanghai.

Zhongguo xiaohuashu qishiyizhong 中国笑话书七十一种,
   Taibei: Shijieshuju.

Zhu Dougou 朱斗荀 1910. *Xiaohua qitan* 笑话奇谭,
   Shanghai.

3

YOUTH AND CULTURE: CINEMA AND YOUTH, YESTERDAY AND TODAY

Giorgio Mantici

Editors' Introduction

Giorgio Mantici has chosen five Chinese films - all produced between 1975 and 1982 - as a basis for discussion of the role of youth in the Chinese society today. First Mantici cuts back to demonstrate two different conceptions of youth maintained in China in this century. One conception he ascribes to Mao Zedong who mainly derived it from his experience in the May Fourth movement in 1919. During this period Mao recognized the power of the young to overthrow the old. In Mantici's opinion this discovery deeply conditioned Mao's later political choices in that he believed that, in any situation, the young are better than the old. A contrasting view upon youth Giorgio Mantici reads in Liu Shaoqi's booklet written in 1939, How to be a Good Communist. Liu stressed a moralistic call for discipline and unity in the party with Confucian connotations and in accordance to the Marxist-Leninist interpretation by Stalin. Liu found little room for a 'new and vital' young generation in the Party. Analysing the five films, Mantici observes a shift in the conception of the youth from 1975 to 1982. This shift coincides with the death of Mao and the political take-over of Deng Xiaoping.

For almost a decade (1966-1976)[1] China was synonymous with rebellious Youth who destroyed the old and tried to build up the new. During that decade, China appeared to the astonished eyes of the West - both to sympathetic observers of what was going on there, and to severer opponents of Mao's regime - the epitome of a youthful nation; the country where the young had managed to grasp (political) power and were now trying to challenge history by giving birth to a new socialist system; one that would be different and opposed to the mode of running the State in the Soviet Union which these young people now denied socialist status: for it was - according to them - nothing but a capitalist state disguised in socialist garments.

Most probably, the Chinese leadership of that time, chiefly Mao Zedong himself, had the intention of backing this image of a Young China which, through a series of uninterrupted revolutionary waves, was building a New Socialist China - not only for the sake of Western observers, but also (and perhaps mainly) for the sake of the Chinese people themselves. We can

see an indirect confirmation of this in the rapid ascent of
the 'young rebel' from Shanghai, Wang Hongwen, to the peak
of CCP leadership.[2] By making the surprising appointment
of Wang Hongwen as Vice-Chairman of the CCP, the 10th
Congress of the CCP appeared to ratify the victory of the
juvenile masses which had been involved during the previous
seven years of the Great Proletarian Cultural Revolution
(GPCR). Wang's mediocre political stature - which we also
had ample opportunity to observe in his not at all brilliant
behaviour during the trial of the 'Gang of Four' - backs up
the hypothesis that his unexpected appointment as Deputy-
Chairman of the CCP could be considered as a sort of prize
given to the generation of 'Revolutionary Rebels' (*geming
zaofanpai*) as a whole. Thus we should see it much more as
having emblematic meaning - i.e. actual political power
given to a young leader because he was a product of the
GPCR - rather than because he had substantial importance.[3]
As everybody knows, the fall of the 'Gang of Four' and the
various political lines which followed one another in the
five-year period between 1976 and 1981 had, firstly, the
effect of damaging and, eventually, of destroying completely
that image of a China filled with young revolutionaries
which the official iconography of the GPCR had made us used
to seeing, and which was considered by many to be both real
and vital. Secondly, they destroyed Mao's utopian vision of
Marxism,[4] of which the GPCR constituted the most outstanding
fruit although, as far as the present Chinese leadership is
concerned, the most disastrous and bitter one as well.[5]

VIEWS ON YOUTH IN CHINA 1915-1965

First, we must answer an apparently trifling question, although one, in fact, central to our analysis: to whom in
China is the term 'young' (*qingnian*) granted? According to
a statement by Mao Zedong, young people are those whose age
lies between fourteen and twenty-five.[6] The discovery of
this age group derives from Mao's experience in the May
Fourth Movement (*Wusi Yundong,* 1919). It was during this
period that he recognized the power of the young as a force
to overthrow the old and usher in the new. This discovery
deeply conditioned Mao's later political choices through his
belief that *in any situation* the new is better than the old,
that *in any situation* the young are better than the old, if
only for their readiness to accept what is new and discard
what is old.[7] This discovery is to be ascribed to the profound influence Chen Duxiu exerted on Mao during this
period and the traces of it are discernible on every single
page of the magazine *Xiang Jiang Ping Lun* which Mao founded

in the summer of 1919, in Changsha, and which he edited and
wrote virtually single-handed.[8]

Mao's generation replied in a very enthusiastic way to the
call to Youth launched by Chen in the pages of the first
issue of his *Qingnian Zazhi*, on 15 September, 1915:

> . . . Youth is like early spring, like rising sun, like
> trees and grass in bud. It is the most valuable period
> of life. The function of Youth in society is the same
> as that of fresh and vital cells in a human body. In
> the processes of metabolism, the old and rotten cells
> are incessantly eliminated to be replaced by the fresh
> and the living . . . If metabolism functions properly in
> a society, it will flourish; if the old and rotten
> elements fill the society, then it will cease to exist
> . . . What is struggle? It is to exert one's intellect,
> discard resolutely the old and rotten, regard them as
> enemies, and as the flood or savage beasts, keep them
> away from their neighbourhood and refuse to be con-
> taminated by their poisonous germs.[9]

I do not think it would be an exaggeration to say that the
metaphor about metabolism, invented by Chen Duxiu, was a
constant companion of Mao throughout his life;[10] that it was
a constant landmark for him in the course of the incessant
(and dialectical) struggle between the new and the old; that
it was a constant encouragement - also from a psychological
viewpoint - and an ideological weapon in his hands, in the
revolutionary struggle as well as in the work of shaping a
New China; and that it was for him a unique choice of life
both as a Marxist revolutionary and, above all, as a *Chinese*
Marxist revolutionary.

Chinese society, in the first decades of this century,
was nothing but an old and rotten social body precisely because it did not allow the young and vital cells of the
country to start up a new process of metabolism which was
the only way to give a new life to that old body. The May
Fourth Youth took upon themselves the task of starting a
process of metabolism so radical that the result was much
more lacerating, long-lasting and hard, than those young
people themselves would have expected and, possibly, desired.

Mao Zedong witnessed and actively took part in such a
process, and he was to keep its profound and indelible mark
for the rest of his life. After the foundation of the CCP
and in a more urgent and marked way after the establishment
of the PRC, the juvenile problem was, mainly, viewed in
connection with the need to channel off the extraordinary
potentialities of Chinese Youth into the political lines
adopted by the CCP. Thus, the problem became extremely

tangled and not at all easy to settle; either one accepted
Youth as a whole with its vitality, its ability to create the
new and in Chen Duxiu's words 'to exert intellect, discard
resolutely the old and rotten, regard them as enemies and as
the flood and savage beasts', and accepted the consequent
potentialities of eversion which it would be difficult to
control, or one had necessarily to dampen, repress, channel
off the 'early spring' into the tracks of a given political
line whenever the targets turned out not to coincide. This
could be done whenever what was old and rotten in the eyes of
Youth was not what was old and rotten, *in a given period,* in
the eyes of the Party; 'to exert one's intellect' meant either
not to accept any imposition at all, or - which could be even
worse - openly oppose the Party line, whenever 'reactionaries'
whom it was right to rebel against, were not the *same*
'reactionaries' pointed out by the Party . . .[11]

From the early thirties Mao Zedong became aware, with an
increasingly radical lucidity, which was the spring of his
political choices in the sixties and seventies, of the
difficulty of dealing correctly with the juvenile problem
when connected with a vast revolutionary project. Nevertheless, he did not forget Chen Duxiu's metaphor about metabolism; he did not forget the importance of the 'new cells'
also in a socialist body: for a socialist body, too, if
choked with old and rotten cells will die. Mao Zedong's
problematical and contradictory approach to juvenile
problems was rather outspoken in his lecture delivered to
Yan'an Youth, on the occasion of the twentieth anniversary
of the May Fourth Movement. According to his view, Chinese
Youth constituted an important army in the anti-imperialist
and anti-feudal struggles, but would only succeed in its
regenerating function on the sole condition that it became
integrated with workers and peasants.[12] Such a statement did
not automatically mean holding back creativity, the capability
of spreading the new and discarding the old, but rather it
implied the need to put all that under the perspective of
'serving the people'. Not only that. The integration of
young people and intellectuals with the workers and peasants
was to be achieved through a new anti-traditional method of
education (i.e. one which opposes the Confucian tradition).
The aim of this was to shorten, little by little, the
distance between labour and intellectual work.[13] Yan'an
Youth espoused such a new method of learning/teaching and
spread it, effectively, and dedicatedly, all over the liberated areas.[14]

Let us, now, dwell upon the position concerning the same
questions, in the same years, of another outstanding Chinese
leader and theoretician of the CCP, Liu Shaoqi. The reason
why Liu's position on Youth and education is worth analysing

lies in the fact that it represented - from the foundation
of the PRC up to the GPCR - one of the most influential
instruments in the field of ideological education. In July
1939, Liu Shaoqi delivered some lectures at the Institute
of Marxism-Leninism in Yan'an, later collected in a booklet,
known in English under the title of *How to be a Good
Communist*. What Liu explained in his lectures - in a very
articulate way, constantly supporting his reasoning with
many quotations from Marxist-Leninist classics - was what
the tasks of a good communist should be; what the correct
attitude of a good communist towards Party work should be;
what mistakes a good communist should absolutely avoid. The
title Liu chose for his lectures was *Lun Gongchandang yuan
de xiuyang* (On the self-cultivation of members of the
Communist Party); they were - quite obviously - directed to
the young Party members, for young Party members were,
mainly, the students of the Institute of Marxism-Leninism
in Yan'an. The basic statement that underlay Liu's entire
reasoning was that a good communist would never start a
debate about the Party line, but would try his best to embody
it and spread it around.[15] Furthermore, Liu's constant and
moralistic call for discipline and unity in the Party, his
reiterating use of the concept of 'self-cultivation'
(*xiuyang*) - the main support of the moral and philosophical
universe of Confucianism - make *How to be a Good Communist*,
paradoxically, on the one hand a quite sophisticated syn-
thesis of both the Confucian and Marxist tradition,[16] and on
the other a doctrinal exposition according to the Marxist-
Leninist interpretation given to it by Stalin. Certainly,
there is a very clear opposition to Mao's *other* Marxism,[17]
that which has been termed Mao's 'Utopian Marxism'. In Liu
Shaoqi's theoretical elaborations there is little room for a
young generation which - being 'new and vital' - could give
its own contribution of 'new cells' to the Party body. The
static, entropic vision of the Party which *How to be a Good
Communist* conveys[18] is, in many ways, opposed to Mao's
dialectical, even conflicting vision of the Party.[19]

Whereas Liu thought of the Party as the only holder of *the*
Truth, an organism which was sound by definition, Mao -
deeply persuaded of the impossibility of avoiding contradictions[20] - thought of it as something that could *even* turn
into an 'old and rotten' organism, thus needing (much more
than any moralistic call to unity and order) those new and
vital cells whose admission would provide it with a new life
and regenerate a sound metabolism, again.

To what extent the Chinese leadership of today is more
inclined to follow an extremely cautious political line -
with respect to the juvenile problem, one which is
possible to correlate with what I would call 'Liu Shaoqi's

line', even if in a very generic sense - comes out in a
quite outspoken way throughout the *Renmin Ribao* editorial
of 5th May, 1979. Herein the sixtieth anniversary of the
May Fourth Movement is commemorated. The direct aim of the
editorial certainly does not seem to be an exaltation of
the young Chinese who in 1919 gave birth to the May Fourth
Movement; Chinese Youth of yesterday and today are not
mentioned once, which cannot fail to seem at least a little
odd, since May Fourth is also celebrated in China as Youth
Day. Instead, the editorial is used as an opportunity to
reinterpret and appropriate *also* the spirit of the May
Fourth Movement in the light of the new policies proposed
by the CCP. In 1979, these were: the mass movement to
'emancipate minds' (*jiefang sixiang*), the race towards the
'Four Modernizations' (*Sige Xiandaihua*), the need for
science and democracy to replace the disastrous ten years
of the 'feudal-fascist' rule of Lin Biao and the 'Gang of
Four'. Not only that. The entire editorial is marked by
constant appeals to patriotism and frequent exhortations to
adopt from the West *only* what is positive and suited to the
real needs of the Chinese people. Thus we find in it no
appreciation whatever of Youth. What is easy to find in the
editorial is a list of rather explicit warnings concerning
what *must* be understood when one is talking about democracy,
science and 'emancipating the minds'.[21]

What comes out rather clearly in the editorial, furthermore, is its distrust (or contempt, even) of Youth, which
should not surprise anybody in a country where the National
Secretary of the Chinese Communist Youth League is a middle-
aged man.

THE ROLE OF YOUTH DURING THE
GREAT PROLETARIAN CULTURAL REVOLUTION

Some Western scholars have rightly pointed out that the
GPCR was, among many other things, a sort of remake of the
May Fourth Movement.[22] Certainly, for almost four years
(1966-1969) Chinese Youth was invested with the role of the
leading character in the most astonishing attempt at a
revolution within a revolution ever to have taken place in
a socialist country. Young Chinese people were also 'used'
by different factions which came to power, in order to
achieve aims that, possibly, left aside the actual interests,
needs and aims of the same young generation. Nevertheless,
the young people have played a leading role on the Chinese
political stage which it would be hard to match in the
history of the PRC before those years and after.

On 21 July, 1966, Mao Zedong, faced with the puzzlement
of the other leading personalities of the CCP over the problem
of giving too much political room to the young, affirms:

> . . . I say to you all: Youth is the great army of the
> Great Cultural Revolution! It must be mobilized to the
> full . . . There were even some (colleges) which
> suppressed the student movement. Who is it who sup-
> pressed the student movement? Only the Beiyang Warlords.
> It is anti-Marxist for communists to fear the student
> movement . . . The Central Committee of the Youth League
> should stand on the side of the student movement. But
> instead it stands on the side of suppression of the
> student movement.[23]

The reference to the Beiyang Warlords is indicative of the
very fact that Mao had clearly in his mind: the equation
'GPCR equals May Fourth Movement'; the urgency and the importance of giving to the Chinese Youth the opportunity to
express themselves freely; the probability that none other
than the young rebels would have dared to follow him and
support him in 'bombarding the Headquarters' (*paoda Silingbu*).
To just what extent Youth was the fundamental landmark during
the GPCR, can be seen from the joint editorial of the *Renmin
Ribao, Jiefangjun Bao* and *Hongqi* of 4 May, 1969, celebrating
the fiftieth anniversary of the May Fourth Movement.[24] If
there is no historical or philological scruple whatsoever,
and the exaltation of the anniversary is openly instrumental,
then, on the other hand, there is a sort of new 'Call to
Youth', a quite frank recognition of the importance of Youth
in the revolutionary struggles of yesterday and today.[25]

A further element of importance in the editorial is the
stress on the anti-feudal nature of the 'May Fourth Cultural
Revolution'. This can be seen in its radical attack on
Confucianism as embodied in the slogan '*Dadao Kongjiadian!*'
(Down with the Confucian Shop); a slogan which had been
coined by Mao's generation.[26]

The editorial then proceeds with a violent criticism of
Liu Shaoqi, and his 'poisonous' booklet on Self-cultivation,
pointing out its manifest Confucian matrix. Thus, for the
second time in this century, Chinese Youth are called upon
to destroy the old; they are called upon to unhinge once
again as during the May Fourth days, the 'national quint-
essence' (in Lu Xun's words), that is the very Confucianism
which has been imbuing Chinese society for almost two
thousand years and even conditioning its socialist choice.
They should feel encouraged in their endeavours by the knowledge that Mao himself stood constantly and openly on their
side. They knew, for instance, that since the late fifties

the Chairman had been scolding the most outstanding leaders
of the CCP for their caution in upholding the new and discarding the old, for their fear of the new and the young.[27]

CINEMA IN CHINA

There are at least two reasons why I have chosen to concentrate on film rather than on any other cultural product.
The first is that cinema is an extremely privileged and
particularly penetrating instrument of ideological propaganda and diffusion. Any film, always, faithfully reflects
the ideology of those who have been involved in the process
of film-making. Moreover, in a Communist country where film-
making is state-controlled and produced,[28] it will inevitably
constitute a direct transmission mechanism for the mass
diffusion of whatever political line has been elaborated at
any given time. The second reason for my choice lies in the
fact that films in China enjoy a three-way system of distribution and diffusion, and thus reach the vastest public on
earth, on an extremely regular basis and with effects which
last far beyond the normal showing or running of the film
itself. The three channels of distribution are first of all
film-shows in cinemas; secondly, broadcasting on television,
often concurrently with cinema showing; and lastly, a comic-
strip version of the film, printed in millions of copies,
sold at a give-away price and available in the bookshops
years even after the film has been released.[29]

Rebellious Youth Depicted in Films, 1974-1977

In this section we will consider rebellious youth in the
GPCR and the 'Gang of Four' period (1974-76) as depicted in
the three films, *Juelie, Chunmiao* and *Qingchun*.

JUELIE (Rupture, 1975) may be considered, among the films
produced in China in the early seventies, as the best example
of a type of political film-making which has been conceived
and produced with the declared aim of serving as an ideological weapon in a continuing political struggle. Furthermore, from a formal point of view, it represents the very
best which Chinese cinematography produced in that decade.
It is impeccably shot, the action is swift and (technically)
skilful and refined, and the actors' performances extremely
good and hardly, if ever, theatrical as often happens in
Chinese films.

The title itself is a declaration of principle: Rupture, indeed, is none other than an explicit reference to a passage in Marx and Engels' *Manifesto of the Communist Party*:

The Communist Revolution is the most radical rupture with traditional property relations; no wonder that its development involves the most radical rupture with traditional ideas.[30]

The theme concerns the revolution in education (*jiaoyu geming*) and, although it is clearly linked to a political campaign still underway at the time of the film's appearance (end of 1975), the story itself is set in 1958, at the time of the Great Leap Forward. This was presumably meant to underline the fact that the struggle known as the 'struggle between the two lines' (*liangtiao luxian de douzheng*) had its origins many years previously and would, moreover, probably concern the masses for many more years to come.

The story-line narrates the first years in the life of the Communist Labour College (*Gongda*) in Jiangxi Province, which was founded in 1958, and the political struggles which characterized its development and which even threatened to bring about its closure.

The main character is Long Guozheng, a revolutionary communist who received his training as a Party member in Yan'an where he attended the Northwest Anti-Japanese Red Army University, known as *Kangda* (Resistance University), and whom the Party has sent to direct the newly founded Communist Labour College of Songshan. The particular characteristic of such a university resided in the fact that, since it was based on the positive experience drawn from revolutionary teaching methods during the Yan'an period, it intended to apply the principle of linking book-learning to productive labour, and scientific research to social practice. Consequently, it represented a radical rupture with old teaching methods. All the classical *topoi* in the struggle between the two lines in matters of teaching are brought out in the film in a succession of exemplary situations which lead up to the inevitable final clash between the young students - who enthusiastically and courageously support the Director Long - and the old professors - perpetrators of the old-style teaching based on book-learning and fact memorization - who have their champion in the Deputy-Director, the tough stubborn old Zao Zhonghe. There are at least two scenes, in which the emblematic value could be immediately grasped by the Chinese audience.

Long Guozheng's arrival in the village occurred on the very day that the entrance examinations for the new college were being held. These examinations were of the traditional

type, and they caused violent protest on the part of the
young peasants who were not allowed to sit for them, because
they did not have the required secondary school diploma.
Long immediately intervened on the side of the young
peasants and openly encouraged them to rebel:

To young Niuzai who complains: 'What can I do? They're all a
bunch of gatekeepers for the bourgeoisie.'

He answers: 'Young fellow, if the bourgeoisie is guarding the
gate, why don't you simply fight your way in?'[31]

Then, Long enters the examination hall and, to the utter dis-
may of the old professors, he invites an old representative
of the poor peasants to sit on the examiners' board. The old
peasant protests at this, saying: 'No, that won't do. A
person in straw sandals like me in charge of enrolment?'

To which Long answers: 'Why not? The Eighth Route Army and
the New Fourth Army wore straw sandals, but they defeated the
reactionaries both Chinese and foreign all the same. We want
precisely someone in straw sandals like you.'[32]

Thus, many young peasants, who do not have a high level of
education, are admitted to the university in accordance with
the Director Long's conviction that:

> If high academic level is required to enter our Communist
> Labour College, then it's simply another way of keeping
> the children of the workers and peasants out. Some
> people say that applicants must have qualifications. What
> qualifications? The bourgeoisie have their qualifi-
> cations and we proletarians have ours. The first quali-
> fication to enter the Communist Labour College is that
> the applicant must be a member of the labouring classes.[33]

The first battle is won by the young people and by Long. The
second paradigmatic scene of the film portrays an amusing
lesson in veterinary surgery. Professor Sun, who had studied
in the Soviet Union, decides to give a lesson on the
importance of the function of horses' tails. It is worth
remembering, at this point, that Jiangxi Province abounds in
buffaloes, and that horses are practically unknown there. A
young and rather foolhardy student - the very same Niuzai
whom Long encouraged to rebel against the 'gatekeepers for
the bourgeoisie' - takes it upon himself to point out the
uselessness of this lesson to the professor, given the fact
that it can have no practical application.

Niuzai stands up. 'I have a question.'
Prof. Sun: 'Fasten your buttons.'
Niuzai buttons his jacket.
Prof. Sun: 'What is it?'
Niuzai: 'Is the college going to send us to Inner Mongolia
to herd horses?'
The other students burst out laughing.
Prof. Sun: 'Be quiet!'
Niuzai: 'You've lectured us on horses for several months.
But horses are rare in this part of the country and in
this mountain region there aren't any horses at all.
Even that plaster model there, which can't neigh or run,
is the first horse I ever saw. Besides, I don't under-
stand you when you lecture.'[34]

The professor throws Niuzai out of the lecture hall, but
Niuzai merely continues his polemic by posting up a *dazibao*
outside the college, saying: 'Lecture less on horses and
more on pigs and buffaloes!'

The film goes on to describe, in passionately sympathetic
terms, successive episodes in the 'struggle between the two
lines'. These, eventually, culminate in a temporary victory
of the academic line, which decides on the closure of the
college. However, at the last moment, in true *deus ex
machina* style, a letter arrives from Chairman Mao, saying:
'Comrades, I am in full agreement with what you have done.'

Needless to say, the Chairman is in agreement with the
young rebels and Director Long. The film is a hymn to those
rebellious Youth who uphold the new and defeat the old order;
and who dare to think with their own heads and to go against
that which they consider to be unjust. It is, also, an open
invitation to Youth to rebel against 'Revisionism' wherever
it is found, always to trust in the masses, and *always* to
support the revolutionary proletarian line of Chairman Mao –
in this case, in the field of education.[35]

CHUNMIAO (Spring Sprout, 1976) is the first Chinese feature
film to deal directly with episodes of the GCPR. The title
is the first name of the film's main character, but it is,
also, an explicit reference to the 'new-born socialist
things' (*xinsheng shiwu*), to the 'sprouts of Communism'
(*gongchanzhuyi de mengya*) springing up all over China
during the GPCR, of which Chunmiao is the incarnation. In
her own words, the actress Li Xiuming, who plays the title
role, expresses it thus:

I wanted to do a good job of acting Tian Chunmiao, as I
was deeply moved by her heroic character. She is a barefoot doctor who serves the people wholeheartedly, a

revolutionary fighter who dares to struggle and knows how
to struggle. She possesses the revolutionary spirit to
go against the tide. As a character she is the incarnation of the militant spirit of the GPCR.[36]

The play takes place in the summer of 1965, in the Hubing
brigade of the People's Commune of Chaoyang in an Eastern
region of China. A peasant woman brings her infant daughter,
who is sick with pneumonia, to the commune hospital accompanied by Chunmiao - who has just returned to her native
village, after having finished her secondary education. The
hospital's doctor, Jian Jiren, who is then far too busy with
some experiments he is carrying out for a personal research
project, keeps the little girl - who is racked by high fever -
waiting, and when he finally does examine her, all he does is
to advise that she be taken immediately to the county hospital. Needless to say, the little girl does not reach
alive. Chunmiao is deeply upset by this whole episode, and
when Chairman Mao launches the directive to concentrate on
rural areas in medical work, she resolves to become a barefoot
doctor (chijiao yisheng) and her brigade sends her to study at
the commune hospital. The political line-up at the hospital
is as follows: on the one side the Director Du Wenjie (a Party
member) and Dr Jian Jiren who oppose the new line in matters
of medical practice; on the other side, young Dr Fang Ming,
who has a regular degree in medicine, and who has especially
asked to be assigned to a rural hospital. Notwithstanding the
patent obstructionism of the two older doctors, Chunmiao
makes excellent progress, thanks also to the constant help of
the young doctor.

She then returns to her brigade, where she sets up a medical centre. In a crescendo of ever more dramatic episodes,
the struggle between the new (Chunmiao, Dr Fang and the other
barefoot doctors) and the old (the Director and Dr Jian, that
is to say the 'capitalist-roaders' zouzipai) becomes increasingly bitter.

Upon the outbreak of the GPCR, Chunmiao launches a violent
attack - consisting of dazibaos and meetings of criticism -
against the 'revisionist administration of the hospital'
(xiuzhengzhuyi guanli). The main episode involves Chunmiao's
decision to admit into the hospital old 'uncle' Shuizhang,
a peasant afflicted with chronic backache, and personally to
take care of him herself. Chunmiao prepares for the old man
an infusion of medicinal herbs, from a recipe which she had
learnt from a doctor of traditional Chinese medicine. Its
immediate effect is to provoke a pain in the old man's legs,
which up until then had been practically without feeling.
Director Du and Dr Jian seize the opportunity to discredit
Chunmiao in the eyes of the peasants, saying that her inex-

perience made the old man worse. Chunmiao sets off to con-
sult the old traditional doctor who tells her that the old
man's pains are a sign of improvement. He does, however,
warn her of the dangers of increasing the strength of the infusion in trying to bring about a quicker recovery. Chunmiao
returns to the village and decides to try out the dosage on
herself, in order to see if it has any negative effects, before giving it to 'uncle' Shuizhang. The situation rapidly
comes to a head when Du and Jian realize that, thanks to
Chunmiao's treatment, old Shuizhang's condition is greatly
improving: this would irreparably ruin their reputation as
professional doctors in the eyes of the masses. So, they
decide to ask a nurse to give the old man an injection under
the pretence of alleviating his pain. Chunmiao arrives just
before the nurse is going to give the old man the injection,
and Dr Jian throws the vial containing the liquid to the
floor to avoid being found out. Chunmiao picks up some of
the glass fragments and takes them to be analysed in the
laboratory. The results confirm her suspicions: the liquid
was none other than a powerful poison.

The old doctors' intention had been to kill 'uncle'
Shuizhang and to have the blame fall on Chunmiao, in order
to discredit the barefoot doctors as a whole. The film's
message is patently obvious: the young (Chunmiao, Dr Fang and
all those young peasants who want to become barefoot doctors)
are the only ones who are ready to support with enthusiasm,
even at the cost of their lives (Chunmiao experiments upon
herself in order to determine the effects of a drug which
could prove lethal), the 'new-born socialist things' (in this
case the barefoot doctors' movement). They are the only ones
with the courage to 'swim against the tide' (*fan chaoliu*) and
to fight steadfastly against the 'revisionist' line of the
'capitalist-roaders' (Director Du and Dr Jian), while knowing
full well that they are engaging in perilous and often mortal
combat. Apart from anything else, such a fight is made more
arduous by the fact that the 'revisionists', the 'capitalist-
roaders' are *in* the Party (Director Du is an old Party
member).

This film, which came out in the early months of 1976, was
vastly successful with the public and the young leading
actress, Li Xiuming, became immensely popular throughout
China.

QINGCHUN (Youth, 1977) although completed after the fall of
the 'Gang of Four', seems to me an ideological product
which - more than any other feature film - represents best the
political line of the 'Four'. Indeed, while both *JUELIE* and
CHUNMIAO fully represent what we might call the 'line of Mao'
- in the fields of education and medicine, albeit slightly

forcing the interpretation to make the political message more
explicit and immediate - *QINGCHUN* represents the ideology of
the 'Gang of Four' in the constantly exasperated extremism of
its interpretation of Mao's directives. If Mao's Marxism
might be said to have connotation of 'Utopianism', under the
interpretation of the 'Gang of Four' it comes to have connotations of religious, theological, abstract and often
delirious fideism. In this sense *QINGCHUN* seems to me an

ang of Four' ideology.
the film had a very
only once on tele-

ntials, is that of a
d paroxysmal volun-
dition. The main
Guard', a deaf-mute,
ng the GPCR, Pang Bai -
p of young comrades
, decide to go on a
order to see Chairman
e part in a huge mass
finally manage to
ally, this is the only
ted extracts from the
e great mass meeting of
ith Chairman Mao
ed Guard' armband, as
of Tiananmen.
strum and one million
f red flags and red
irman Mao!' (*Mao*
she is the only one
airman by joining the
his is such a shock to
e village, she decides
al treatment (mostly by
se of her voice and
rongly motivated that
ost completely normal
e end of the story.
operator . . .
Bai reading, with
an see from the cover)
artyrs of the Revol-

ution' (*geming lieshi*); she is particularly struck by the
story of a deaf-mute communist fighter who dies for the
Revolution. At that precise moment, a violent storm damages
the telephone lines and a team of workers gets ready to go
out into the night and into the storm to locate and repair

the damage. Pang Bai insists on joining the team, and when
they find the severed wire, it is she who climbs up the telephone pole and, at great risk to her life, takes hold of the
two ends with the almost fatal consequence of inevitable
electric shock.

Why do I consider this film to be, in every respect,
exemplary of how the 'Gang of Four' reduced the 'line of Mao',
in the final analysis, to a series of behavioural formulas
which were both absurd and decidedly religious? As I see it,
the story seems to suggest the moral that through unbridled
revolutionary subjectivism and ardour, sustained by the mere
vision of the Chairman, one is able to overcome any obstacle
whatsoever (even the impartial laws of Physics: electric
current in our case). However, this is not the only reason.
It also proposes the 'martyrs of the Revolution' - and
martyrdom, obviously - to the young generation as a model of
behaviour and it suggests that it is necessary, in order to
build a socialist society, to be prepared to sacrifice one's
life, even when the particular act of sacrifice itself is
both stupid and pointless.

Socialist-Confucianist Youth Depicted in Films, 1981-1982

The recent trend in Chinese cinema seems to portray a rather
more socialist-confucianist and slightly xenophobic youth.
This is best seen in the two films *XI YING MEN* and *MUMA REN*.

One of the major screen successes of 1981 was *XI YING MEN*
(The Joy Returns to the Family, or The In-laws), the most
explicit attack, so far, on the young generation's lack of
respect for its elders to have ever been launched through the
Cinema screen.

It is a (realistic) fable-like tale, which narrates the
story of the day-to-day problems of living together in a
peasant family in Northern China. The difficulties brought
about by different generations sharing the same house are
exemplified through the story of two young sisters-in-law,
one of whom is 'good' (Shuilian, whom we see in the first
scenes marrying Chen Renwu, a production-team leader) and the
other 'bad' (Qiangying, the wife of Renwu's elder brother,
Renwen).

The 'bad' one - 'bad' because she is egoistical, although
a hard worker and a very good housekeeper - tries from the
start to convince the 'good' one that she must stand up to
their mother-in-law. In one scene, which is both 'amusing'
and chilling at the same time, at least for a Westerner who
has been historically influenced by the feminist culture of
the last decade, we see Qiangying trying to convince Shuilian
to attack their mother-in-law for the sake of a piece of

forcing the interpretation to make the political message more explicit and immediate - QINGCHUN represents the ideology of the 'Gang of Four' in the constantly exasperated extremism of its interpretation of Mao's directives. If Mao's Marxism might be said to have connotation of 'Utopianism', under the interpretation of the 'Gang of Four' it comes to have connotations of religious, theological, abstract and often delirious fideism. In this sense QINGCHUN seems to me an absolutely exemplary product of the 'Gang of Four' ideology. And this is, possibly, the reason why the film had a very short run in cinemas and was broadcast only once on television.

The story-line, reduced to its essentials, is that of a 'miracle' invoked by an exasperated and paroxysmal voluntarism, in the purest hagiographic tradition. The main character of the film is a young 'Red Guard', a deaf-mute, who lives in a mountain village. During the GPCR, Pang Bai - the name of the heroine - joins a group of young comrades who, not at all unusual for those days, decide to go on a 'long march' of their own to Peking in order to see Chairman Mao. When they reach Peking, they take part in a huge mass meeting in Tiananmen Square where they finally manage to catch sight of the Chairman. Incidentally, this is the only Chinese feature film to have incorporated extracts from the period documentary film which shows the great mass meeting of 18 August, 1966, in Tiananmen Square with Chairman Mao wearing his green PLA uniform and a 'Red Guard' armband, as he greets the crowds from the rostrum of Tiananmen.

When the Chairman appears on the rostrum and one million 'Red Guards', in a sea of exultation of red flags and red booklets, begin to cry: 'Long Live Chairman Mao!' (Mao Zhuxi Wansui!), Pang Bai realizes that she is the only one who cannot show her devotion to the Chairman by joining the others in their cries of adoration. This is such a shock to her that, when she returns to her native village, she decides to undergo a lengthy and painful medical treatment (mostly by acupuncture) in order to acquire the use of her voice and hearing. Needless to say, she is so strongly motivated that she is able, in the end, to achieve almost completely normal speech and hearing. But that is not the end of the story. Pang Bai decides to become a telephone operator . . .

A key scene of the film shows Pang Bai reading, with mounting emotion, a book which (as we can see from the cover) narrates the exemplary lives of some 'martyrs of the Revolution' (geming lieshi); she is particularly struck by the story of a deaf-mute communist fighter who dies for the Revolution. At that precise moment, a violent storm damages the telephone lines and a team of workers gets ready to go out into the night and into the storm to locate and repair

the damage. Pang Bai insists on joining the team, and when
they find the severed wire, it is she who climbs up the telephone pole and, at great risk to her life, takes hold of the
two ends with the almost fatal consequence of inevitable
electric shock.

Why do I consider this film to be, in every respect,
exemplary of how the 'Gang of Four' reduced the 'line of Mao',
in the final analysis, to a series of behavioural formulas
which were both absurd and decidedly religious? As I see it,
the story seems to suggest the moral that through unbridled
revolutionary subjectivism and ardour, sustained by the mere
vision of the Chairman, one is able to overcome any obstacle
whatsoever (even the impartial laws of Physics: electric
current in our case). However, this is not the only reason.
It also proposes the 'martyrs of the Revolution' - and
martyrdom, obviously - to the young generation as a model of
behaviour and it suggests that it is necessary, in order to
build a socialist society, to be prepared to sacrifice one's
life, even when the particular act of sacrifice itself is
both stupid and pointless.

Socialist-Confucianist Youth Depicted in Films, 1981-1982

The recent trend in Chinese cinema seems to portray a rather
more socialist-confucianist and slightly xenophobic youth.
This is best seen in the two films *XI YING MEN* and *MUMA REN*.

One of the major screen successes of 1981 was *XI YING MEN*
(The Joy Returns to the Family, or The In-laws), the most
explicit attack, so far, on the young generation's lack of
respect for its elders to have ever been launched through the
Cinema screen.

It is a (realistic) fable-like tale, which narrates the
story of the day-to-day problems of living together in a
peasant family in Northern China. The difficulties brought
about by different generations sharing the same house are
exemplified through the story of two young sisters-in-law,
one of whom is 'good' (Shuilian, whom we see in the first
scenes marrying Chen Renwu, a production-team leader) and the
other 'bad' (Qiangying, the wife of Renwu's elder brother,
Renwen).

The 'bad' one - 'bad' because she is egoistical, although
a hard worker and a very good housekeeper - tries from the
start to convince the 'good' one that she must stand up to
their mother-in-law. In one scene, which is both 'amusing'
and chilling at the same time, at least for a Westerner who
has been historically influenced by the feminist culture of
the last decade, we see Qiangying trying to convince Shuilian
to attack their mother-in-law for the sake of a piece of

material. Needless to say, 'good' Shuilian does not fall into
the trap. However, the scene which is most exemplary - and
which aroused indignation in the peasant masses to whom the
film's success was due - is certainly the one where Qiangying
is seen preparing, for her husband and children's supper, some
jiaozi (dumplings). In the meantime, her husband's grand-
father, whom the poor woman is obliged to look after by decree
of her husband's family clan, has come home. She hides the
jiaozi and only gives the old man some corn-bread for supper.
After further similar 'provocations' Qiangying out of desper-
ation decides to leave her husband's house and she goes with
her children to her own parents' house. This causes much indignation among the members of the Chen family clan and Renwen
threatens Qiangying with divorce. It falls to Shuilian, of
course, to get her 'bad' sister-in-law to come back home; all
is forgiven and forgotten and the clan is once more united and
(un)happy.

The Confucian essence which permeates the entire story is
evident and proudly paraded: it is the duty of the young to
respect and care for the old. The peasant family institution
has its good, venerable traditions and they must not only be
respected but also preserved and handed down. In the words
of the film scriptwriter:

> People told me that general morality in the villages had
> deteriorated mainly as a result of the ten-year turmoil
> of the 'Cultural Revolution'. Family quarrels, ill-
> treatment of parents, disputes between brothers and
> sisters and divorce suits had increased. Fewer young
> couples still lived with their parents. Many newly-weds
> immediately moved to separate quarters. Some regarded
> parents as a burden which they tried to throw off. Thus,
> many families disintegrated, leaving a number of old
> people helpless and alone . . . I wanted to write a film
> dealing with these contradictions in a realistic way and
> presenting good solutions based on actual life . . . I
> wanted it to promote social morality, restore some fine
> traditions and help to build up our socialist spiritual
> civilization.[37]

Matters are slightly more embarrassing as far as 1982's enormous screen success, *MUMA REN* (The Herdsman), is concerned.
In fact, among the other 'fine Chinese traditions' proposed
again to the audience, we also find a subtle hint of xeno-
phobia, in this case of an anti-American sort.

The story tells of a father, Xu Jingyou, and a son, Xu
Lingjun, who meet again after almost thirty years of separation. The father had left China and his wife and son,
straight after Liberation, and now he has returned as a rich

capitalist and the president of an American chemical company. During the more than twenty years that he has been away many things have happened; his wife has died and his son has been brought up and educated by the State. After becoming a primary school teacher, Lingjun was condemned in 1958 as a 'Rightist' because of his 'American' father; and he has been sent to the Northern grasslands to herd horses. Xu Lingjun carries out his work most conscientiously and in so doing becomes aware of the realities of rural China. He marries a young peasant girl with whom he has a son and he continually has to put up with all manner of injustices and humiliations because of having been branded as a 'Rightist'. After the fall of the 'Gang of Four', his case is re-examined and finally he has the label of 'Rightist' (*youpaitiezi*) removed.

The 'Peking Hotel', where father and son meet again, is described from an overtly condemnatory viewpoint with regard to the foreigners who live there (who, by the way, are constantly surrounded by bottles of 'Johnnie Walker', even in the toilets). The father is presented in decidedly unsympathetic terms, for his sole purpose in returning to China is to find his son and to take him back with him to America, where he can offer him a life of ease and wealth.

However, the herdsman prefers to return to his prairies and his peasant wife and baby son. The father leaves for America alone, quite contented. After all, he has been able to see for himself just how much his son and the society he represents have become estranged from his own 'modern', 'American' way of life.

An Italian student, who was in *Beida,* told me that the film created some tension between the foreign students and their Chinese *tongwu* (room-mates). Indeed, whereas the former did not identify themselves at all with the 'foreigners' portrayed in the film (by the way, one secondary character in the film says that among other strange customs, American young people are used to dancing in the nude . . .), the latter did identify themselves to quite an extent with Xu Lingjun.

Quite clearly, such a film tries to project to Chinese Youth a decidedly negative image of the Western way of life, which in recent years has come to be a dreamt-of model to follow. And so, *MUMA REN* is a 'perfect' film in this sense. It has a multiple message: the China of today is not only able to repair the errors of the past (the campaign against the 'Rightists', the GPCR, oppression of the 'Gang of Four'), but also it can offer the young better models for living (i.e. models which turn out to be more *moral*, at least) than those in the West. Thus, the young Chinese of today should have faith in the New Socialist China which with all its shortcomings is still far better than any Western society.

CONCLUSION

Our analysis of the cultural model presented in the films examined here makes it extremely difficult to answer such an important question as: 'And tomorrow's Youth?' Certainly, the problem of Chinese Youth today is both delicate and complicated. There are a number of unanswered questions which spring to mind:

How far is the fresh proposal of the traditional Chinese family linked to behavioural norms rooted in Confucianism, with its rigid and canonical rules, reconciliable with a plan for a new and modern socialist China by the end of the century? How will young Chinese be able to distinguish the 'good' things of the West and throw out only the 'bad' things? Who is most useful to the modernized China of tomorrow: the 'good' respectful and Confucian Shuilian or someone like Chunmiao who is ready to embrace the new and destroy the old?

The challenge which we referred to at the very beginning, was lost both by Mao and the Red Guards. History usually leaves no room for appeals; it limits itself to recording what has happened; and whatever happens it goes on. Chinese Youth of today has returned - or rather has been forced to return - to a very Chinese starting point, that is: to be respectful towards old people, to be respectful of the learned, to study in a very conscientious way, to work hard - as usual - for socialism, to serve - as usual - the people. It would not be easy either to guess or to predict what will happen in the near future. For the moment, young Chinese people seem to be - apparently, at least - very controlled and calm. What will be worth observing in the immediate future is *how* Chinese Youth will react to those patterns of culture imported from the West. Not only in their gaudiest behavioural aspects, which until now has meant taking pride in having long hair - and quite often artificially curled; wearing, at night even, sun-glasses whose shape is supposed to be western-like; sporting, with proud daring, 'trumpet-like' blue-jeans (as the Chinese expression *laba kuzi* describes them). But, most importantly, what will be the impact of all the stimuli (both ideological and cultural) which will be brought back by the significant number of young Chinese sent abroad by the government to study in Western universities in recent years?

One final question might be raised: what will happen if these 'returned students' of today - who will possibly form the bulk of the Chinese leadership of tomorrow - are able to initiate a real process of modernization that does not co-incide with the socialist modernization which the leadership of today wish to promote? Will they be able to start a 'new' May Fourth Movement?

Certainly, there is a real risk, at the moment at least. Lu Xun, in 1927, wrote a bitter 'random note' which reads: John Stuart Mill says that tyrannies make men become cynical. What he did not know was that republics make men become silent.' Tomorrow this might read: 'But he did not know that People's Republics make the young become both cynical and silent.'

APPENDIX

JUELIE
(*kupture*, other English title *Breaking with Old Ideas*)

Director:	Li Wenhua
Screenplay:	Jun Zhao, Zhou Jie
Production:	Beijing Film Studio, 1975.

CHUNMIAO
(*Spring Sprout*)

Director:	Xie Jin
Screenplay:	Zhao Zhiqiang, Yang Shiwen, Cao Lei
Production:	Shanghai Film Studio, 1976.

QINGCHUN
(*Youth*)

Director:	Xie Jin
Screenplay:	Li Yunliang, Wang Lian
Production:	Shanghai Film Studio, 1977.

XI YING MEN
(*The Joy Returns to the Family*, other English title *The In-Laws*)

Director:	Zhao Huanzhang
Screenplay:	Xin Xianling
Production:	Shanghai Film Studio, 1981.

MUMA REN
(*The Herdsman*)

Director:	Xie Jin
Screenplay:	Li Zhun
Production:	Shanghai Film Studio, 1982.

1. I indicate the 1966-76 decade not because I accept the official dating proposed in the *Resolution on certain questions in the history of our Party since the foundation of the PRC,* which was unanimously adopted by the Sixth Plenary Session of the Eleventh Central Committee of the CCP on 27 June, 1981, but because it constitutes a period which bears the marks of political choices which are all linked to the theoretical elaborations of Mao's last years.

2. Wang Hongwen, born in Shanghai in 1936, was the youngest Vice-Chairman of the Party since the foundation of the PRC. He was 37 when he was appointed to the position.

3. The prestigious position of Vice-Chairman of the CCP, conferred on Wang Hongwen is what is known as *chuanli* in Chinese political jargon, that is to say: power deriving solely from the importance of the position one has. Indeed, he had no *shili* (i.e. effective personal power as a politician apart from that conferred upon him by his position), let alone *weixin* (vast popular support). See Steve S.K. Chin (ed.) *The Gang of Four. First Essays after the Fall,* University of Hongkong, Hongkong 1977.

4. The definition is S.R. Schram's and it is to be found in Stuart R. Schram: 'To Utopia and Back: A Cycle in the history of the Chinese Communist Party', *The China Quarterly,* no. 87, September 1981, pp. 407-439.

5. See *Resolution on certain questions . . .* in *Beijing Review* no. 27, 6 July, 1981, pp. 10-39. For the Chinese text cf. *Renmin Ribao,* 1 July, 1981, pp. 1-5.

6. Cf. Mao Zedong, 'Qingnian tuan de gongzuo yao zhaogu qingnian de tedian' (The work of the Youth League must consider the characteristics of Youth), in *Mao Zedong Xuanji,* vol. V, Beijing 1977, p. 84.

7. E. Collotti-Pischel, 'Considerazioni sul rapporto tra Mao Zedong e i giovani', *Cina,* no. 16, Roma 1980, pp. 19-41.

8. Cf. G. Mantici (ed.), *Pensieri del fiume Xiang,* Editori Riuniti, Roma 1981.

9.   'Jinggao Qingnian', *Qingnian Zazhi,* no. 1, vol. I, 15
     September, 1915, p. 1; for a version in English cf.
     Ssu-yü Teng and J.K. Fairbank, *China's Response to the
     West,* Harvard University Press, Cambridge (Mass.) and
     London, 1979, pp. 240-6.

10. One need only remember a famous quotation of Mao's,
     which is none other than a paraphrase of Chen Duxiu's
     metaphor on metabolism:

          A man is supplied with arteries and veins that,
          through the heart, put the blood into circulation;
          he breathes with lungs, breathing out carbon dioxide
          and breathing in fresh oxygen; that means discarding
          what is rotten and absorbing what is new. A
          Proletarian Party, too, must discard what is rotten
          and absorb what is new, and only in this way will it
          be able to be full of dynamism. If the Party does
          not discard the rotten and absorb new blood, it will
          be lacking in dynamism. Cf. 'Xishou wuchanjieji de
          xinxian xieye' in *Hongqi* no. 4, 1968, p. 7.

11. It will be sufficient to recall two episodes. On 10
     November 1974, a *dazibao* appeared in Guangzhou entitled
     Democracy and Legality in Socialism and signed Li Yi
     Zhe. It constitutes the hardest, best-documented and
     most creative criticism of the so-called 'Lin Biao
     System' and of the 'Gang of Four', not only when the
     latter was firmly in power but long before the very
     expression 'Gang of Four' had even been coined. This
     dazibao was branded as 'counter-revolutionary' and its
     authors imprisoned. Five years later, when the politi-
     cal climate had changed, the official press greatly
     exalted the revolutionary daring of the three Cantonese
     and they were not only released from prison but also
     held up for the young people of the whole country as
     heroes and defenders of socialist democracy. In
     September 1980, the Third Session of the Fifth
     National People's Congress adopted a resolution to
     eliminate from the Constitution the right, among
     others, of writing big-character posters. One wonders
     how the young heroes will manage in the future to ex-
     press their views and defend socialist democracy.
          In the first week of April 1976, The Monument to
     the Martyrs of Revolution situated in the centre of
     Tiananmen Square was the setting for a series of popular
     demonstrations. The demonstrators were mostly young
     people and students: their purpose, on the one hand, was
     to commemorate the late Premier Zhou Enlai on the

Memorial Day for the Dead (*qingming jie*), and on the other to criticize most violently and courageously the 'Gang of Four' and its (mis-)management of power. It was like stepping back in time to the days of 4 May, 1919: young people addressing the passing crowds, reading poems which had been written especially for the occasion . . .

On 7 April, the *Renmin Ribao* published an editorial which branded the demonstrations as 'counter-revolutionary incidents' (cf. *Hsinhua News Agency*, 8 April, 1976, no. 6589, p. 3).

At the end of 1978 the Central Committee of the CCP decided that the Tiananmen incident was to be considered as absolutely revolutionary.

12.   'Qingnian yundong de fangxiang' (The Orientation of Youth Movement), in *Mao Zedong Xuanji*, Beijing 1969, pp. 529-30.

13.   Mao Zedong, 1969, ibid.

14.   Cf. M. Selden, *The Yenan Way in Revolutionary China*, Harvard University Press, Cambridge (Mass.), pp. 267-74.

15.   Cf. Liu Shaoqi, 'How to be a Good Communist', in *Three Essays in Party-Building*, Foreign Languages Press, Beijing 1980, pp. 18-19.

16.   It is interesting to note that the judgement concerning the Confucian essence of Liu's argumentations is pointed out long before the 'Red Guards' or the GPCR, by Western scholars. See H.G. Creel: *Chinese Thought from Confucius to Mao Tse-tung*, University of Chicago Press, Chicago 1953; Etiemble: *Confucius*, Club francias de livre, Paris 1956. For the debate on Liu's book during the GCPR, see J. Daubier, *A History of Chinese Cultural Revolution*, Vintage Books, New York 1974, pp. 180-2; D. Milton and N. Dall Milton, *The Wind Will Not Subside: Years in Revolutionary China 1964-1969*, Pantheon Books, New York 1976, pp. 69-70, 221-3.

17.   For an alternative view of the Liu/Mao relationship to the one I profess, see the illuminating passages in Schram, op.cit., *passim*.

18.   Liu Shaoqi, op.cit. p. 91-6.

19.   Schram, op.cit. p. 439.

20. S.R. Schram (ed.), *Mao Tse-tung Unrehearsed - Talks and Letters: 1956-71,* Penguin Books, Harmondsworth 1974, pp. 107-8.

21. Cf. *Beijing Review,* no. 20, 18 May, 1979, pp. 8-11.

22. Cf. M. Meisner, 'Cultural Iconoclasm, Nationalism and Internationalism in the May 4th Movement', in B. Schwartz (ed.), *Reflections on the May 4th Movement,* Harvard University Press, East Asia Research Centre, Cambridge (Mass.), 1972, pp. 14-22; S.R. Schram, 'From the "Great Union of the Popular Masses" to the "Great Alliance"', *The China Quarterly,* No. 49, January-March 1972, pp. 88-105.

23. Schram (ed.), 1974, op.cit. pp. 253-4.

24. The text contains numerous references to articles by Mao written in the thirties and forties, and which the reader is warmly invited to study and meditate upon.

25. English translation in *Peking Review,* no. 19, 5 May, 1969, pp. 20-2.

26. English translation in *Peking Review,* ibid.

27. Schram (ed.), 1974, op.cit. pp. 118-20.

28. There are, in China, seven film production companies, situated in the major Chinese cities (Peking, Shanghai, Changchun, Guangzhou, Xi'an and Chengdu), including the PLA production company *Ba Yi* (1 August) which is also in Peking. The film industry is all State-run; the only instance of an 'independent' film production in contemporary Chinese cinema is *Yuanye* (The Wilderness or Wild Land, 1981), by Lin Zi. It must be noted, however, that this film has never been released in China, and that the director herself was not able to explain to me what an 'independent' production might actually mean in China today.

29. In charge of it there is in China one publishing house, the *Zhongguo Dianying Chubanshe,* which is located in Peking. I wish to express my gratitude to Dr. Marco Müller who kindly put at my disposal the richest bibliography available in Italy on the Chinese film industry. It is only thanks to his friendship and kindness that I had the opportunity to read the original Chinese screenplays of the feature films with which I shall deal.

The main reference books on Chinese cinematography in Western languages are: J. Leyda, *Dianying. An Account of Films and Film Audience in China,* Cambridge (Mass.), and London: The MIT Press, 1972; A.Bergeron, *Le Cinéma Chinois. I/1905-1949,* Lausanne: Alfred Eibel, éditeur, 1977; W. Eberhard, *The Chinese Silver Screen, Hongkong and Taiwanese Motion Pictures in the 1960s,* Taipei: The Orient Cultural Service, 1972. The most useful reference book in the Chinese language is *Zhongguo Dianying Nianjian* (Chinese Cinema Yearbook), Beijing: Zhongguo Dianying Chubanshe, 1981, 1982 . . .

30. K. Marx, F. Engels, *Manifesto of the Communist Party,* Foreign Languages Press, Peking 1972, p. 57.

31. From the original screenplay by Jun Zhao and Zhou Jie, cf. *Chinese Literature,* No. 6, 1976, p. 17.

32. Ibid. pp. 25-6.

33. Ibid. p. 25.

34. Ibid. pp. 36-7.

35. Cf. C. Pozzana, 'Un'arma di lotta per la rivoluzione dell'insegnamento: il film 'La Rottura' (Juelie)' *Vento dell'Est,* No. 41, Anno XI, Marzo 1976, pp. 170-5.

36. Cf. Li Hsiu-ming (Li Xiuming), 'Acting a Barefoot Doctor on the Screen', *China Reconstructs,* Vol. XXV, No. 6, June 1976, p. 39.

37. Cf. 'New Creation in the Countryside', in *China Reconstructs,* no. 5, May 1982, p. 47.

4

CHINA'S CHANGING IMPORT POLICIES
FOR THE ELECTRONICS INDUSTRY

Detlef Rehn[+]

Editors' Introduction

In the last few years, China's import policy for the electronics industry has undergone fundamental changes. The reasons for these changes may be found in the import policy of the 1950s and 1960s which is discussed in the opening paragraphs of Detlef Rehn's article. The announcement of the modernization goals led to massive imports in 1978-9, but they were not based on a strategy which would select the items to be imported according to the short and long-term needs of China's electronics industry. This situation changed substantially only in 1980-1, when developmental goals for the electronics industry were fixed. Elements of the policy have resulted in a mixture of imports of plants, equipment and single items, based on a strong assumption of the Chinese capacity for quick absorption of the imported technology. The global emphasis on consumer electronics has been a driving force in the development of the electronics industry. Top priority is now on the components sector: emphasis on mini-computers and microcomputers, and on consumer electronics will play an important role for the whole electronics industry. The implications of these goals are discussed at length. In the closing paragraphs, Detlef Rehn suggests the institutionalization of a system of experts who will be responsible for the development of the electronics industry, and reforms in the planning system.

In a speech given in April 1981 at the Peking Computer Factory No. 3 on the occasion of a meeting to test a newly-developed minicomputer, the DJS-140, Li Rui, head of the State Administration of Computer Industry (*Guojia Jisuanji Gongye Zongju*) said that one of the reasons for the backward state of China's computer industry is the blind and uncoordinated importation of computers from abroad. 'If we do not control the imports and take measures to protect our own national computer industry, we will very probably collapse', he said.[1]

In October 1982, it was known that the Shanghai Computer Factory, the leading Chinese producer of computers, had to stop the production of table calculators, because calculators were bought abroad in large quantities. For the same reason

---

+) I am indebted to J. Delman, Aarhus, and C. Rabe, Bonn, for valuable comments.

Also, the production of the DJS-051 microcomputer, which
started in the end of 1978, had to be given up in the enterprise mentioned.[2]

On 15 October, 1982, the *Xinhua Ribao,* the provincial news-
paper of Jiangsu Province, announced the completion of a plant
for the production of picture-tubes for colour and black-and-
white television sets.[3] The plant has been set up in Wuxi
(Jiangsu Province) and was established by the Japanese enterprise Toshiba at a price of around US$58 million.[4] High-
ranking Chinese officials attended the inauguration meeting,
which certainly underlined the importance of the project;
among others, there were Wang Bingshi, Vice-Governor of
Jiangsu Province, and Jiang Yimin, Vice-Minister of the
Ministry of Electronics.

The two examples seem to contradict each other: on the one
hand, the Chinese authorities attempt to control imports of
foreign equipment and technology, which is a logical outcome
of the Shanghai example; on the other hand China engages in
the massive importation of new plants for the electronics
sector. But a more careful analysis will show that there
has been a fundamental change in China's attitude towards
foreign electronics technology, and that import restrictions
and plant purchases are both elements in the new import
policy. Other aspects of this new policy include the strong
awareness on the part of Chinese planners of the need for
quick absorption of the imported technology, of a careful
analysis of foreign experiences, and - as compared to past
policies - of a stronger emphasis on consumer electronics
which is now regarded as an important factor for the future
development of China's electronics industry. In the following
I shall discuss these aspects in detail.

FOREIGN TECHNOLOGY IN CHINA'S ELECTRONICS INDUSTRY - AN HISTORICAL SURVEY

To understand the new policy it is necessary to go back to
the period prior to 1980. From the early beginnings foreign
technology played an important role in the establishment of
China's electronics industry. Both in Research and Development (R&D) and in manufacturing there was a strong foreign
influence, mainly from the Soviet Union and other East
European countries. In the early fifties China imported
four major plants for the electronics sector from the Soviet
Union and the GDR to manufacture components, radios and telephone equipment.[5] The purpose was to establish initial
production capacity and to get access to foreign expertise in
the field.

As China's electronics industry was practically non-existent at that time, importation of complete plants was a necessary step which contributed to the establishment of a sound basis for development. Along with the plants, expertise was also transferred to China.

Moreover, leading Chinese electronics experts who had been educated in the West returned to China in the late 1940s and 1950s. Among others, there were Huang Kun, PhD, Bristol University, 1948, currently Director of the Institute of Semiconductors, Chinese Academy of Sciences (CAS); Wang Shouwu, PhD, Purdue University, 1949, currently Vice-Director of the Institute of Semiconductors, CAS; Lin Lanying (f), PhD, University of Pennsylvania, 1955, currently Vice-Director of the Institute of Semiconductors, CAS; Lü Baowei, PhD, Harvard University, 1947, currently Chairman of the Chinese Society of Wave Transmission.[6]

As these Chinese specialists were probably familiar with the most recent technological development in the West, their knowledge as well as the newly-established research and production facilities created favourable conditions for rapidly developing China's electronics industry. For example, as early as 1964, Huang Kun, Wang Shouwu and other semiconductor experts in the Semiconductor Institute of the Academia Sinica built China's first integrated circuit (IC). At that time, the gap between China's computer technology and that of the West was just a few years.

The withdrawal of Soviet experts in 1960 forced China to change its import policy, and China turned to the West to satisfy its need for imported technology. But instead of going on purchasing complete plants, only single items were imported. This change in the structure of imports seems to be due to both the export controls exerted by Western countries, as well as to China's fear of becoming technologically dependent upon the West, as it had been in the fifties on the Soviet Union and other East European countries.

According to Reichers,[7] Chinese imports from the West amounted to a total value of US$206.6 million between 1960 and 1970, of which US$116 million were used for professional and scientific instruments and apparatus, US$25 million for telecommunication equipment, US$61 million for electric measuring and controlling instruments, and US$3 million for electronic tubes, photo cells and semiconductors. The imported items were supplied by Japan, West Germany, the United Kingdom, France, Switzerland, and the Scandinavian countries.

Apparently, these imports had a very positive effect on China's electronics industry. Szuprowicz[8] notes that during these years China's electronics sector made substantial progress and by acquiring Western technology instead of developing its own technology it saved considerable time.

Being the focal area within China's electronics industry,
military electronics in particular underwent rapid development in the 1960s. This is not surprising as the bulk of
the imported foreign technology most likely was channelled
into the military sector, and absorption was facilitated
because of the high concentration of manpower skills in this
sector.

However, the situation within China's electronics industry
changed significantly after 1970. The reasons for this are
manifold:

First of all, the 'steel versus electronics' debate which
took place in 1970-1, and which centred around the question
whether electronics or steel should be given priority in the
process of developing the national economy, had an immediate
impact on the electronics industry[9] as the result of the
debate was a call for simultaneously developing all economic
sectors with 'steel as the core' (*yi gang wei gang*). Consequently, electronics had to serve this political dictum.
One result was that the imports of foreign electronics technology dropped considerably for some years; another more
important result was that it remained unclear until 1978
which role electronics should play in China's economic
development.

Secondly, the decentralization of economic decision-making
in the early 1970s not only led to the establishment of a
large number of new, mostly small, electronics enterprises,
but also to the establishment of 'independent systems' within
the electronics industry in many Chinese provinces. Hence
the electronics industry experienced overlapping imports of
electronics technology, and often a very low capability of
absorption because of inter-provincial differences in technological level and performance.

Thirdly, as the result of a rising technological standard
within the electronics industry in the 1960s, the demand for
higher sophistication of the imported technology grew as well.
However, a national system of experts, with responsibility for
deciding upon what was actually needed in China's electronics
industry in the long perspective, was almost lacking entirely
until 1977. Furthermore, the vertical structure of the electronics industry prevented the harmonization of different
approaches towards the importation of foreign technology. But
even after a decision was made on unifying and controlling
imports, there was no apparent indication of the decision
being actually carried out. For instance, around 1972-3,
China imported NOVA-1200 minicomputers from Japan to function
as blueprints for the design of its own DJS-100 minicomputer
series. Although this was a very important step for the
development of China's computer industry, many problems arose
when it came to developing and producing the first computer

in the series, the DJS-130, as there was no uniform design for it. Instead, the absence of a national design institution, which could formulate the relevant design parameters to attain full compatibility between domestic and foreign computer systems, often led to differences in the computer architecture worked out by the participating research and production units. The consequence has been that even today lack of compatibility is still one of the most serious problems within China's computer industry.

Fourthly, the dichotomy between military and non-military electronics has become more and more apparent. While military electronics was the focal point of development in the 1960s, with the result that imported foreign technology was primarily channelled into the military sector, non-military application of electronics technology became more and more important in the 1970s. Consequently, the need for foreign technology within the non-military sector became even more apparent. One example is the draft of the DJS-100 minicomputer series which was clearly aimed at non-military application.

The main features of China's policy for importing technology for the electronics industry before 1978 may be summarized as follows:

- The uncertainties about the role of the electronics industry in the process of developing the Chinese economy led to competition among planners within the electronics industry and those within other branches of the economy for the limited funds available for purchasing foreign technology.

- Within the electronics industry itself priorities had not been defined as yet, and there were hardly any institutions on the national level to co-ordinate import activities according to clearly formulated strategic conceptions. Consequently, there was a state of permanent competition between the military and civilian sectors within the electronics industry, between research and production sectors, between the central and the provincial level, etc.

- The organization structure of the electronics industry, which was strongly verticalized, prevented any effective absorption of the imported technology.

THE SITUATION IN 1978-79

The first elements in the new import policy for China's
electronics industry can be dated back to 1978, when it was
made clear that the electronics industry was to be one of the
key sectors in China's modernization programme. Furthermore,
there is evidence to prove that foreign technology is to play
a decisive role in developing the electronics branch. Hence,
at the outset of the modernization policy in 1978 there was a
massive increase in the imports of foreign electronic technology. All kinds of technology were bought abroad; and the bulk
of the imported items went into non-military industrial electronics aiming at enlarging the basis of the electronics industry. Consumer electronics benefited from the modernization
policy as well. Not only did China import large quantities of
television sets and other consumer electronics goods, but also
production facilities (plants and production lines) for manufacturing picture tubes and other basic components. This
step indicates on the one hand a shift away from purchasing
prototypes exclusively, and on the other hand, the replacement
of imports with the products of China's own gradually developed consumer electronics industry.

In particular, computers were on the top of the import
list. This is not surprising as the computer industry is regarded as one of the weakest links in China's electronics industry. It is still a problem, however, that a lot of different foreign computer systems have been purchased and applied
in the various sectors of the Chinese economy for quite a
number of years, especially in 1978-9 when computer imports
reached a peak level. This has left China with the problem
of a lack of compatibility between domestic and foreign computer systems, a problem urgently needing to be solved (see
Table 1). One reason for this import of different systems is
that the Chinese government has feared becoming too dependent
on one kind of technology or on one country's technology.
Another reason is that, quite obviously, various Chinese
institutions were able to import computers uncoordinatedly
according to their own needs, as long as these were in line
with the overall modernization policy (see Table 2).

Undoubtedly, China made real efforts to develop the electronics industry in 1978-9, but the goals seem all in all to
have been far too ambitious. Emphasis was put on what was
considered the most advanced technology without taking into
consideration the potential applicability of this technology.
The state-of-the-art of the electronics industry was not
evaluated. Short-term as well as long-term development goals
were not formulated; this would have resulted in selectively
importing only 'strategic' items. Consequently, problems

Table 1. Distribution of imported computers: countries, enterprises, and models, China, 1956-79

Country	Enterprise	Model	Quantity
USA	DEC	PDP-8, 11	20
	VARIAN	620/L-100	14
	WANG	2200	14
	DGC	NOVA	9
	HP	9800, 2100	8
	Other		46
USA, total			111
Japan	Shimadzu	NOVA	23
	Hitachi	CT, DCP	10
	Hokushin	HIDIC, M	9
	Other	HOC	6
Japan, total			41
			89
France	Telemechanique	Solar	6
	Intertechnique	Multi	6
	Other		17
France, total			29
West Germany	Siemens	7700, 330	11
		CP 550	15
West Germany, total			26
UK, total			9

Table 1: (continued)

Soviet Union and 4 other East European countries, total	18
4 West and North European countries, total	12
Total imports	294

Source: China Computerworld, 28 February, 1981

*Table 2: Domestic and foreign computers in different
sectors, China, 1979*

Sector	Number of computers used	of which: foreign computers
Machine-building	586	76
Science and education	499	51
Metallurgy	399	69
Energy	243	21
Light and textile, chemical industries	188	15
Traffic, post and telecommunications	173	6
Culture and health	112	4
Geophysics	74	15
Industrial and planning statistics	43	15
Agriculture, forestry, meteorology	37	10
Other	200	12
Total	2604	294

Source: China Computerworld, No. 3, 1981

concerning absorption of the acquired technology could not be solved either.

On the other hand, in the process of reorganizing the electronics industry, the Chinese government did take some important steps: specialized societies were restored, the State Administration Bureaux for the Computer Industry and for the Radio and TV Industry were institutionalized, and the China Electronics Import & Export Corporation was established. Furthermore, various industrial corporations were founded on the provincial level.

ELEMENTS OF THE NEW CHINESE IMPORT POLICY IN THE ELECTRONICS INDUSTRY

In order to overcome the resulting disproportions which emerged in striving for an overall modernization of the electronics industry, the Chinese authorities defined the following developmental goals around 1980-1:[10]

Firstly, top priority be given to the development of the components sector.

Secondly, in the computer industry emphasis be placed on the development of mini- and microcomputers.

Thirdly, consumer electronics be given an important role in the development process.

Having learned from studying foreign experiences, China now strives for a narrow integration of imported technology with domestic production structures, and for a quick absorption of imported technology as well.[11]

In comparison with China's past policy for developing an electronics industry, some new and very interesting aspects reveal themselves: the reason for giving priority to the components sector is to be found in the backwardness of this sector in China; the components sector is regarded by the advanced countries (Japan, USA, etc.,) as the key sector in the electronics industry, as well as the sector with the most rapid technological progress within the entire electronics industries as such.

Furthermore, the emphasis on minicomputers and microcomputers, and in particular on mutually compatible serial computers, shows that large-scale production of computers and widespread computer application in all sectors of China's industry and within China's society as a whole, is a focal point in economic modernization.

The growing importance of consumer electronics reflects the ambitions of Chinese electronics planners to satisfy the increasing popular demand for consumer electronics goods. It is believed that the consumer electronics sector may give the necessary impetus for the development of an overall electronics industry within China because it would demand the mastery of the basic manufacturing technology required in the production of guaranteed, high-quality parts and components. Radios, TV sets and tape recorders would have to be mass-produced. The mastery of basic mass-production techniques would solve the problems the Chinese have had until now with the production of newly-developed products.[12]

Finally, the call for a narrow integration of imported technology with production and for a quick absorption of the acquired technology shows that China is now willing to overcome one of the maladies of the past, namely that of importing technology for its own sake without considering factors like feasibility and applicability. Again it seems likely that Chinese planners have studied very carefully Japan's positive experiences with acquiring and absorbing foreign technology.[13]

As for the composition of electronics imports, some very important changes took place after 1980-1. Until around 1976, there was a one-sided emphasis on the importation of single items; in 1978-9, imports of finished products (TV sets, computers, etc.) became more and more important. But the Chinese authorities soon became well aware that one-sided emphasis on the importation of finished products is not a rational solution for developing China's electronics industry, either.

Since 1980-1, the import policy of China's electronics industry, therefore, has emphasized mixed imports of expertise, manufacturing technologies, prototypes, plants, and finished products. In the following, I would like to show how the new import policy is carried out in the areas mentioned above, i.e., within the components sector, the computer industry, and the consumer electronics sector.

Components are the basis for all sectors within the electronics industry.[14] Although in research, China has reached some very good results, for instance the development of a 16 K RAM IC[+), announced in 1982, lack of co-operation between research institutions and producers has resulted in a very poor level of manufacturing for many years. At present, the highest density of integration of ICs under production in China is 4 K, and the yield rates[15] are very

---

+) K: kilobit; RAM: random access memory; IC: integrated circuit.

low. The given figures may also be compared with current
trends in Japan and the United States where 64 K RAM are
being produced, and 256 K RAM are at present in the process
of development.

As far as production is concerned, the most important
reasons for the backwardness of China's components industry
are low level of automation, partly outdated equipment, poor
management techniques, low educational level of labour, and
basic problems in the understanding of manufacturing techniques.

Another more general, but equally important, reason for
the present backwardness of the components sector is that
the decentralization of economic decision-making and planning
around 1970-1 dislocated the components industry. IC producers are now found all over the country, naturally in
Beijing and Shanghai, but also in Gansu and Guizhou. This
lack of concentration of production facilities in a technology-intensive branch like the IC industry seems to prevent
any substantial technological progress.

To overcome this problem the Chinese government recently
decided to establish IC (LSI)[+) centres in North China,
including Beijing, Tianjin and Shenyang, and in South China,
including Shanghai, Jiangsu and Zhejiang provinces.[16] This
seems a reasonable measure as these cities and provinces are
among the most important centres within China's electronics
industry as such and, according to Chinese standards they
all require a high concentration of research and production
which is an important condition for the development of the
IC industry.

On the other hand, the Chinese are well aware that they
need foreign support for developing their components
industry as the technological gap between China and the West
in this area has widened significantly because of the
enormous technological progress in the components sector of
advanced countries.

At present, one priority area is the construction of
plants to produce semiconductor components for colour
TVs.[17] The Wuxi facility, mentioned in the introduction to
this paper, is the first in a series of such plants. One
section of the Wuxi project is made up of imported US equipment for producing wafers for integrated circuits which are
going to be assembled in the Toshiba plant. I think that
the advantages of the project include: access to modern manu-
factoring technology which will have an impact on the development of the entire Chinese components industry; new management

---

+) LSI: large-scale integrated circuits.

methods which will help to organize IC production in a much
more efficient way than is the case today; better quality TV
sets which will undoubtedly influence the production of
domestically-designed TV sets; a rising level of competitive-
ness as far as Chinese products entering the world market are
concerned. The Wuxi facility will serve as one of the back-
bones for developing new IC centres in the future.

A factory in Luoyang under the Ministry of Metallurgical
Industry is another important components producer which will
use modern foreign technology for the manufacture of mono-
crystalline silicon wafers. The equipment has been imported
from the United States and it includes equipment and materials
for a clean-room, and a crystal pulling furnace.[18] While
Chinese imports for the components sector are still fairly
limited because of Western export controls (COCOM), the
situation is completely different for the less sensitive
consumer electronics sector. As for consumer electronics,
foreign technology plays its most important role within the
TV industry. After substantial Chinese imports of television
sets from 1978 to 1980, in early 1981 the State Council
decided to restrict these imports in order to protect the
emerging Chinese TV industry. Today, emphasis is on the
importation of complete plants to acquire expertise and manufacturing techniques for mass-production of TV sets for the
Chinese as well as the world market. According to the *China
Business Review* the facilities which until now have been
mainly imported from Japan include: plants for assembling
colour TV sets and colour picture tubes (Hitachi), plants
for producing flyback transformers for colour TV sets (Sanyo),
a black-and-white TV assembly-line (Hitachi), a black-and-
white picture tube assembly-line (Matsushita), a black-and-
white television glass bulb production facility (Corning
Glass, US), etc.[19] Most of these went into production in
1981 and 1982.

In China's computer industry emphasis is now on mini- and
microcomputers, and this tendency is expected to continue in
the near future.[20] Imports include Intel and other microcomputer systems for application in universities, research
institutes, and factories.[21] Adding a declining volume in
the importation of mainframes to these purchases it seems
that today China's import policy in the computer field is
related to actual needs and based on a clearly formulated
development path, whereas in the past all kinds of computers
were bought abroad, often without any clear notions as to
where and how to use them.

Apart from the imports of complete systems, various
microprocessors (Z-80, M6800, Intel 8080, etc.) are imported
as well. They serve as important elements in the emerging
Chinese microcomputer industry.

The decisive aspect behind all imports is the question of how quickly the acquired technology can be absorbed. The potential for absorbing foreign technology is probably still very weak in the Chinese components industry. The technology for manufacturing integrated circuits is very complicated, and the Chinese still lack experience with imported equipment. Moreover, there is a long way to go from absorption of technology in one plant to developing potentials for absorption in the whole branch. In this connection the problem of internal technology transfer has to be solved. Some of the problems, however, could be solved through the establishment of the above-mentioned IC centres for North and South China, which would mean concentration of Research and Development and production facilities, and of an experienced and well-educated staff.

Furthermore, the establishment by the United Nations Development Project (UNDP) of an Information Processing and Training Centre in Beijing for the computer industry could come out as one of the most important projects for the further development of China's electronics industry because it attempts to tackle the most crucial aspects of absorption, the educational level of the labour force. The same is true with the establishment of software training centres by Japanese enterprises[22] through which the Chinese will gain access to modern software technology.

CONCLUSIONS

Undoubtedly, China's import policy in the electronics industry has undergone important changes over the last few years. However, to bring these changes into full effect, reforms have to be carried out as well within the Chinese administrative and economic system. They would include:

Firstly, an institutionalization of a system of experts who can shoulder the responsibility of developing the electronics industry. Convening conferences of experts where crucial issues in the development of the different sectors within the electronics industry are discussed and where plans for development are drafted would be one step in this direction.

Secondly, reforms in the planning system. Import plans should not only fix quotas and norms for purchases abroad, but should also encompass the absorption of the acquired technology.

If these reforms are carried out, one may expect the electronics industry to play the role envisaged at the outset of the modernization policy. The information that China is to export 1,000 BCM-III single-board microcomputers - a mixture of Chinese and foreign technologies - to West Germany at a price 25 per cent cheaper than similar systems abroad, indicates China's future foreign trade potential in the field, as well as the role to be performed by foreign technology in China's computerization.

Future development of China's electronics industry will certainly be a very interesting topic for analysis.

NOTES

1. Li Rui: 'Zou lianhe de daolu - nuli fazhan wo guo de dianzi jisuanji gongye' (Take the path of combination, develop actively our computer industry), in: *Xiaoxing Jisuanji Yu Yingyong* (Minicomputer and Application), No. 3, 1981, pp. 1-5.

2. 'Lu chan dianzi jisuanji zenyang dakai chulu' (How to open a way for Shanghai's computers), in: *Shijie Jingji Daobao* (World Economic Herald), 18 October, 1982.

3. 'Jicheng dianlu zhuangpei yinjin gongcheng zai Wuxi touchan' (An imported facility for IC assembling put into operation in Wuxi), in: *Xinhua Ribao,* 15 October, 1982.

4. Value given by *The China Business Review,* January-February 1982.

5. Szuprowicz, B.: 'Electronics', in: Orleans, L.: *Sciences in Contemporary China,* Stanford, 1980, pp. 435-61.

6. Cheng Chuyuan: *Scientific and Engineering Manpower in Communist China, 1949-1963,* U.S. Government Printing Office, Washington, D.C., 1965, Appendix IV.

7. Reichers, P.: 'Electronics Industry in China', in: U.S., Congress, Joint Economic Committee: *People's Republic of China: An Economic Assessment,* U.S. Government Printing Office, Washington, D.C., 1972, pp. 86-111.

8. Szuprowicz, op. cit.

9. For a description of the debate cf. Sigurdson, J.:
    *Technology and Science in the People's Republic of
    China*, London, 1980, pp. 124-5.

10. 'Zhongguo dianzi gongye', in: *Zhongguo Jingji Nianjian,
    1981*. (Almanac of China's Economy 1981), Beijing,
    1982, pp. IV-79-IV-83.

11. 'Riben jixie gongye de zhenxing he ke jiejian de jing-
    yan' (The rapid development of Japan's machine-
    building industry and the lessons which may be drawn
    from it), in: *Jixie Zhoubao* (Machine-Building Weekly),
    No. 93, 25 June, 1982.

12. For a general description of these problems cf. Rehn,
    D.:*Betriebliche Forschung und Entwicklung und Inno-
    vationsprobleme in der chinesischen Elektronik-
    industrie*, unpublished manuscript, April 1982.

13. *Jixie Zhoubao*, No. 93, 25 June, 1982.

14. In the following paragraphs I shall only consider
    integrated circuits, not diodes, transistors, etc.

15. Because of technical reasons (purity of materials,
    cleanliness of the air etc.) some of the chips under
    production have to be rejected. The yield rate gives
    the percentage of 'good', i.e. usable, chips produced
    from the wafer, a (silicon) slice. The higher the
    technological level of chip production, the higher is
    the yield rate. Yield rates of Japanese 4 K RAM are
    probably near to 100 per cent, while the Chinese rates
    reach only 10 or 20 per cent or even less.

16. *Guangming Ribao*, 25 December, 1982.

17. Part of the information in the following paragraphs is
    taken from Brown, C.: 'Semiconductors', in: *The China
    Business Review,* May-June 1982, pp. 45-8.

18. ibid.

19. Habegger, J.: 'TV Production: Interference in the
    Industry', in: *The China Business Review,* January-
    February 1982, pp. 25-8.

20. Berney, K.: 'China's Computer Revolution', in: *The
    China Business Review* November-December 1981, pp.14-21.

ibid., p. 16.

Cf. *Far Eastern Economic Review,* 3 December, 1982: 'Hard facts about Japanese software'.

5

CADRES: FROM BUREAUCRATS TO MANAGERIAL MODERNIZERS?

Tony Saich

Editors' Introduction

In China 'red' and 'expert' have been used to describe the correct balance required in order to be a cadre. Though Mao and Deng both came to the same conclusion that a high quality of the cadre force was essential to the implementation of their policies, they disagreed about the methods which should be used to ensure the quality. To Mao, cadre policy was to be aimed at preventing revisionism by means of increased study of Mao's thought, and by bringing the cadres under mass supervision to prevent them from becoming 'divorced from the masses'. Today the main guarantee to ensure that cadres behave properly is to make rules and regulations governing their behaviour. Tony Saich in his article discusses the new requirements for cadres following the death of Mao Zedong. Saich demonstrates that the cadre policy since 1976 can be divided into two periods. While Hua Guofeng essentially tried to limit the number of cadres under attack since December 1978, the emphasis has been for the cadres to acquire professional and scientific competence. From 1980 Deng Xiaoping emphasized the need for cadres to be younger and more specialized and professionally competent, and also stressed the problems of the organizational system such as lifetime tenure for cadres and the over-concentration of power. In the last part of his article Tony Saich analyses a range of problems which have confronted the present leadership: the number of old cadres with but few technical skills, the overstaffing of the bureaucracy, and the increased opportunities for corruption by cadres due to the current policies of 'economic liberalization'. Finally, the impact of the administrative reforms on cadre policy is discussed. To Saich, a crucial problem remains whether the educational system can be expanded rapidly enough to train sufficient quantities of people to the required levels.

> Cadres[1] are a decisive factor, once the political line is determined . . . In the final analysis, leadership involves two main responsibilities: to work out ideas, and to use cadres well (Mao Zedong, 1938).[2]

As the current leadership group centred around Deng Xiaoping has consolidated its grip on key positions of power and policy direction, it has increasingly focused its attention on the organizations and people who will implement the policy. Indeed in any system once policy has been decided it is necessary to have an efficient set of administrators to fulfil and enforce policy. In fact, the administrators can play a crucial role prior to this stage by providing the basic information on the basis of which decisions are made. However, in the Chinese system, not only are these administrators to be efficient; they must also display a political commitment to the policies they pursue.[3] Consequently, political criteria have always played an important part in the selection of the Chinese cadre force.

However, the desire of all China's leaders to create a modernized and socialist state has meant that performance criteria cannot be ignored entirely. In fact as Kautsky has observed, the pursuit of economic development and the values required therein have clearly been in conflict with the values required to maintain revolutionary fervour and momentum.[4] Instead of selecting committed revolutionaries to run the bureaucracies, the emphasis switches to trying to find technically skilled managers to preside over the economy. In China this conflict is seen most acutely in the discussions over both recruitment and promotion of personnel. The dichotomy is referred to by the Chinese as the need to strike a correct balance between a cadre being sufficiently 'red' and 'expert'. More recently these two components have been referred to as 'political integrity' and 'professional competence'.

For Mao this balance created a problem, less so for his successors. Those whom Mao considered most politically reliable, for example workers and peasants, tend to fare rather badly when judged by the criterion of technical and professional competence. To compound the problem the reverse has also proved to be the case. Those whom Mao eyed with most suspicion, for example intellectuals and technicians, tend to be those with the necessary skills to push the economy forward. Such a problem does not present itself to the current leadership. They have actively sought the support of the intellectuals and technicians, stepping up their recruitment into the Party and leadership positions, improving their living and work conditions and even defining intellectuals as an integral part of the working class.

More than its predecessors, the current Chinese leadership has rested its claim to legitimacy on its economic performance and, in particular, on its ability to improve living standards. The attempt to achieve the 'four modernizations' is felt to require changes in organization and a change in the type of person who staffs the organization. Now as in the early fifties and early sixties greater stress is being placed on the technical skill of cadres. Ideological outlook is not ignored but current interpretations of the guiding ideology have been tailored to suit the present stress on modernization. While ideological education is still strongly emphasized for Party members and Party cadres, greater freedom has been accorded to non-Party cadres and non-Party intellectuals. To meet their objectives the current leadership is seeking to bring about the 'four transformations' of the cadre force aimed at making it more revolutionary, younger in average age, better educated, and more professionally competent. Many of the older cadres are held to lack an understanding of the complex problems now facing them, and to cling to old methods for trying to solve new problems.

The renewed emphasis on technical skills is reflected in the Party Constitution adopted at the Twelfth Party Congress, September 1982. The first-listed duty for Party members relates to both ideological and professional work. It calls on Party members to 'conscientiously study Marxism-Leninism and Mao Zedong Thought' and to 'acquire general scientific and professional knowledge'.[5] This is in marked contrast to the previous three party constitutions which only refer to ideological affairs for the first duty of Party members.

The remainder of this article will consider the evolution of the current cadre policy before looking in more detail at the most important problems identified by the current leaders and the proposed solutions.

Finally, a preliminary assessment will be made of how effective these reforms may prove to be.

THE EVOLUTION OF CADRE POLICY SINCE THE 'GANG OF FOUR'

Very simply, cadre policy since the arrest of the 'Gang of Four' can be divided into two periods, although each period exhibits countervailing tendencies and fluctuations. The dividing line is drawn to coincide with the convening of the Third Plenum of the Eleventh Central Committee, December 1978. This Plenum announced the significant shift in the focus of work to economic modernization. Class struggle was no longer considered the principal contradiction in Chinese society, and the struggle for production has been placed in the centre of the stage. Consequently, the major task for cadres is to implement the new economic policies. Yet clearly opposition remained and the new policies have created some new problems.

Following the arrest of the 'Gang of Four' the main focus of attack was centred, not surprisingly, on weeding out their supporters within the cadre force. Under Hua Guofeng's leadership the initial intention was to limit the number of cadres under attack. Although endemic features, such as corruption and waste, were criticized their existence was directly attributed to the influence of the 'Gang of Four' and their manipulation of the continuing feudal ways of thinking. The problems of bureaucracy were laid at the feet of the 'Gang of Four'. This had the beneficial effect of restricting the extent of the purge, as the cadres were given an escape route and the chance to try again. The extent and persistence of general administrative incompetence was not yet acknowledged and neither were the structural causes of these problems such as the 'lifetime tenure' system for cadres. With respect to recruitment, Mao's line was re-affirmed, i.e. politics or revolutionary qualities were still in command.

During 1978 the focus of criticism began to shift. The increasing number of 'returned cadres' who had been purged during the Cultural Revolution led to a widening of attack both in terms of the numbers of cadres criticized and the origins of the behaviour criticized. In March 1978, the *People's Daily* called for the rectification campaign to be extended to all government units in the country. It also called for people guilty of a number of sins, not directly connected with support of the 'Gang of Four', to be removed from office.[6] Following this the Chinese media published an increasing number of articles concerned with corruption, bad work-style, lack of production expertise, etc., among the cadre force. The exposés of corruption were clearly designed to give credence to the claim that China would now abide by the principles of democracy and socialist legality rather than following what the leadership saw as the arbitrary principles governing the years of rule by the 'Gang of Four'. While factionalism, a code-word for opposition, among the cadre corps was still criticized it was no longer seen as the major problem. By mid-1980 Hu Yaobang was commenting that if factionalism did still exist it was far less than was reported. Hu still thought that the greatest problem lay with the cadre force and its feudal mentality. However, rather than claiming that this problem was a product of the 'Gang of Four's' rule or something which they exploited, its existence was seen as one of the reasons for the 'Gang of Four's', and Lin Biao's, rise to power.[7]

In June 1979, Hua Guofeng pointed out the need to improve the cadre force. To make cadres more accountable to the masses he stressed the role of elections and opinion polls. To improve their quality he called for the establishment and improvement of 'systems concerning the examination, assessment, supervision, reward and punishment, removal, rotation and retirement of cadres'. With respect to this last point he singled out the 'iron-rice bowl' practice which meant that, irrespective of performance, cadres could carry on in their jobs.[8] In addition, however, he gave assurances to those cadres currently serving in their posts. Through retraining followed by examinations which would provide an 'important criterion' for promotion or upgrading, incumbent cadres would be given the chance to improve their skills.[9]

These themes were developed by Ye Jianying in September 1979. While stressing that most incumbent cadres simply required retraining, he called for the gradual increase in recruitment of younger and middle-aged cadres and those with more specialized training.[10] He emphasized that it was 'impossible to give competent leadership to modernization efforts if one does not study hard and acquire scientific knowledge'.[11] An important part of this process would be the reduction in the 'general run of administrative cadres' and the increase in the number of specialist cadres.[12]

Increasingly structural problems were being identified as a major source of the cadres' poor performance. In August 1979, the *People's Daily* noted that, 'Some problems are caused by irrational regulations which provide privilege for cadres far beyond their needs and far above their average living standards'.[13]One year later an article in *Red Flag* also traced part of the problem to 'our own institutions'. This article stated that the fault arose because of 'the creation of an unwieldy political superstructure, the major problems of which are the practice of lifetime tenure for cadres and the practice of higher ranks expecting and receiving greater privileges'.[14]

Deng's January Report

These emerging strands were drawn together in two talks by Deng Xiaoping in 1980. However, they were drawn together in such a way that would give little comfort to incumbent cadres. In both his January report and his August speech Deng briefly referred to the need for cadres to have the correct political outlook; in January he simply referred to the need to uphold the four principles, and then centred his attention on the need to improve professional competence and to promote younger people. In August he emphasized the need for cadres to be better qualified, younger and more specialized and professionally competent - a formula which amounted to only three of the four transformations which were to become later policy, the 'more revolutionary' having been excluded.[15] While acknowledging that many problems were connected with the 'thought and workstyle of certain leaders'[16] he claimed that problems of the organizational system, such as lifetime tenure of cadres and the over-concentration of power, were also to blame. In January, Deng put forward his view of the relationship between being 'red' and 'expert'; an interpretation which put greater emphasis on the expert side of the relationship. With respect to selection and promotion Deng emphasized the need to concentrate on those around forty years of age. The significance of this age-group is that they are people who were educated and who graduated between 1949 and the start of the Cultural Revolution.[17]

The thrust of Deng's statements was echoed by Song Renqiong, the Head of the Party's Organizational Department. Song stated that an increasing number of leadership positions should be reserved for graduates of universities and secondary technical schools only, and that emphasis should be placed on the selection of cadres who were young and middle-aged people of a high cultural, scientific and technical level.[18] In December 1980, a special commentator in the *People's Daily* condemned previous cadre practice, and quoted Hu Yaobang in support of the new technocratic ethos. The writer quoted Hu as having said that in future cadres should not, in general, be recruited directly from 'the workers and peasants with a low level of education'.[19]

Such a policy emphasis would bring little comfort to many incumbent cadres who had little or no formal educational qualifications or had those which were considered little better than useless, as they were gained during the Cultural Revolution decade (1966-76). Older cadres were reluctant to retire, while those recruited during the years 1966-76 were reluctant to see their promotion opportunities disappear. Consequently, the reform programme ran into considerable opposition. In September 1980, Hua Guofeng, as he had done before, made a plea on behalf of the incumbent cadres. Again he called for incumbent cadres to be allowed to receive training at specialized schools or on specialized courses either while on duty or during periods of leave.[20]

The opposition led to the adoption of a more flexible approach to the application of age and education requirements, the granting of more extensive retraining opportunities to incumbent cadres and giving retiring cadres a greater say in selecting and training their successors. In particular the article made concessions to cadres recruited during land reform. The article stated that they should not be kicked out because of their low educational level but, given three years training, they could still give another ten years work.[21] In addition to the criteria of making the cadre force younger, better educated and more professionally competent a fourth aspect was added to make it more revolutionary. This aspect re-emphasized the need for continued political training and a correct ideological standpoint. This

was seen to favour the older cadres who, while not possessing
the formal educational requirements, could point to a long
revolutionary record. However, the criterion of being more
revolutionary has been increasingly interpreted as simply
supporting the policy initiatives and political line ushered
in since the Third Plenum. With respect to those recruited
during the years 1966-76 it was made clearer which were the
categories of people whose services would no longer be required. Among others Chen Yun has pointed to three categories
of people who should be removed from their posts. These are
people who had risen to prominence in the Cultural Revolution
by following the 'Gang of Four' in rebellion; people who are
seriously factionalist in their ideas, and people who in-
dulged in beating, smashing and looting.[22]

Problems and Solutions

Both Mao Zedong and Deng Xiaoping came to the conclusion that
the quality of the cadre force was the major stumbling-block
to the implementation of their policies. They even agreed on
the nature of some of the major problems but they disagreed
about the nature of the fundamental problem and about the
methods which should be used to cure the problem. On the eve
of the Cultural Revolution Mao, while agreeing that corruption and ossification of the cadre force were indeed
problems, felt that these were not the major problems. The
major problem concerned revisionism, and the bureaucracy and
those working in it were the main source giving rise to it.
Consequently, as Harding has shown, while Mao did not wish
to destroy the bureaucracy he did attempt to create a bureaucracy and cadre force which would be more responsive to his
policies, more efficient and more ideologically committed.[23]
Cadre policy was to be aimed at preventing revisionism. This
was to be aided by increased study of Mao's thought and by
bringing the cadres under mass supervision to prevent them
from becoming 'divorced from the masses'. An important part
of this process entailed the cadres transforming themselves
and their way of thinking in order to make themselves more
responsive to the new demands placed upon them. It is clear
that such an approach differs from that currently employed
but it is similar to that adopted by Hua Guofeng in the first
couple of years after Mao's death. Behind the attributing of
cadres' problems to faulty work-style lay the implicit
assumption that what was primarily needed was for cadres to
liberate themselves from their bureaucratic and feudal ways
of thinking. Such an approach does not find accord with
that outlined above. Now the main guarantee to ensure that
cadres behave properly is to devise rules and regulations

governing their behaviour, etc., and to try to make sure that they are adhered to. Cadre behaviour will be monitored by institutional bodies such as the Party Commissions for Inspecting Discipline and the People's Procuratorates rather than by direct mass supervision.

Old Cadres: Rehabilitation and Retirement

The major set of problems concerns the fact that the present cadre force is too old with too many only having general administrative skills and too few with specialized, technical skills. The overstaffing of the bureaucracy with those lacking specific skills is seen to arise directly from the system of lifelong tenure. An article in the *People's Daily* pointed out that only 'death and wrong-doing' could lead to the demotion or dismissal of a cadre.[24] Another *People's Daily* article indicated the 'evils' which sprang from this adherence to the lifelong tenure for cadres:

> Personnel in leading posts tend to be senile . . . it is difficult for talented and erudite people to be recruited to leading bodies and get experience . . . the system does not encourage people to work hard but muddle along . . . nepotism replaces appointment on merit . . . power tends to become highly concentrated until ultimately all powers of the Party and State are wielded by one person alone.[25]

Part of the blame for the excessive number of older, poorly-trained cadres lies, ironically, with Deng Xiaoping and his supporters. Under the slogan of 'Seek Truth from Facts' and the corresponding policy of 'correcting mistakes whenever they are discovered', verdicts were reversed on a whole set of people criticized from the mid-fifties, many of whom returned to swell the ranks of the bureaucracy. Some idea of the magnitude of the problem can be gleaned from the statement of Deng Xiaoping's that 2.9 million people were re-habilitated because of wrongful victimization by the 'Gang of Four'.[26] Because the return to work of many of these people was not accompanied by a purge of a corresponding number of Cultural Revolution recruits, it caused a surge in the number of officials at all levels. This gave added impetus to the need to trim the bureaucracy while at the same time increasing the potential opposition to such trimming.

Clearly, the most important policy initiative with respect to this problem has been the decision to abolish the system of lifelong tenure for cadres. It is hoped that such an initiative will make cadres more accountable and

more liable to dismissal should they prove to be incompetent
or corrupt. The Fifth Plenum of the Eleventh Central
Committee[27] formally acknowledged that the system would be
terminated, and this was reflected in the new State and
Party Constitutions. However, the measures finally adopted
were 'watered down' in comparison with the original intentions. For example, the Party Constitution, while pointing
out that cadres were not entitled to lifelong tenure, contained no stipulations strictly limiting the term of office.
An earlier draft which was circulated contained greater details concerning both the period of tenure and the average
age limit for cadres.[28] Hu Qiaomu stated that 'after re-
peated discussions' it was decided that strict limits on the
term of office would not be set. The reason Hu gives is
that it is necessary to retain some veteran cadres with
experience and high prestige to ensure 'stability and
maturity' of leadership.[29]

An integral part of this policy is the attempt to intro-
duce a system for retirement. Unless the older cadres can
be persuaded to retire the attempts to promote better
qualified, younger cadres are clearly doomed to failure.
Song Renqiong cited the age problem along with the lack of
specialist skills as the two major problems with the cadre
force. He called the 'phenomenon of aging' serious and
commented that leaders at the various levels are now twenty
years older than they were before the Cultural Revolution.[30]
In mid-1982 an article in *Red Flag* reported on the question
of the age of the leaders and some of the consequences. It
claimed that 'in some provinces the average age of the
secretaries and deputy secretaries of provincial committees
is above sixty; a large proportion of the cadres of county
committees are fifty-six or older'. This situation meant
that 'many cadres are always ill. They cannot work eight
hours a day, have to be hospitalized or must rest at home
from time to time'.[31] At the end of 1982 eighty-six per
cent of the country's twenty million cadres was said to be
between twenty-six and fifty-five.[32]

The attempt to persuade cadres to retire has led to
appeals to their good nature, the introduction of regulations, and offers of financial inducements. In March 1982,
the *People's Daily* informed veteran cadres that their
'glorious and sacred duty' was to retire! This, it was
stated, was the greatest contribution that one could make in
one's old age.[33] Such appeals, however, are not sufficient.
Song Renqiong[34] called for retirement to be carried out in
accordance with Central Committee regulations concerning the
method for reckoning age and for only those specially required to stay on.[35] To help make use of the expertise of
cadres once retired and to make them feel of use, the post

of adviser has been set up in most Party and State bodies.
Finally, financial incentives are to be made available to
those who do retire. According to the Hong Kong paper *Ming
Pao,* government cadres at or above grade thirteen of the
administrative scale will receive on retirement their normal
salary plus an additional one yuan for every year worked.[36]

Ideology and Replacement

While persuading the old and infirm to stand aside it must
be assured that the people who replace them and that those
who remain in their posts are sufficiently qualified. In
his January Report, Deng Xiaoping pointed out the severe
shortage of trained cadres while *Red Flag*, in the same year,
pointed out the low level of qualification of the leaders.
Red Flag stated that few cadres were really proficient in
professional work, that many were lay people and that some of
these people were in leading positions making final decisions
at the provincial level.[37] Towards the end of 1982 rough
statistics on the educational level of the twenty million
cadres were quoted. It was claimed that 58.7 per cent had an
educational level of senior-middle school or above.[38]
Conversely over forty per cent of the cadre force had not
even attained this not especially high level. The problem is
particularly acute at the basic levels, and particularly in
the rural areas basic-level cadres have been singled out for
their inability to deal with the technical aspects of agriculture. The cause of this problem in the rural areas is
traced not only to the low levels of education of the commune
cadres but also to the organizational system in the countryside. Cadres were expected to undertake the work of both
economic organization and government organization. This
meant that not only did cadres have little time to devote to
gaining professional and technical skills but also that they
had little incentive. As most were paid by the State irrespective of economic performance there was little reason to be
unduly concerned about improving local economic performance.[39]
 If the incumbent cadres do not possess the necessary
vocational skills one would presume that at least their knowledge of ideology and Party history is fairly sound. However,
not even this seems to be the case. *Red Flag* reported the
poor results attained by propaganda cadres in tests during a
training course for philosophy instructors. Only twenty per
cent of the cadres could give satisfactory replies to four
questions on basic philosophy; about forty per cent did very
poorly and some even handed in blank papers; and twenty-
five per cent had not been able to answer a question about
the Party's ideological line. Apparently some did not know
what the Third Plenum had been about, and questions about

basic Party history had produced some 'outstandingly wrong answers'.[40]

Three solutions are put forward to help deal with the problems of the shortage of skilled personnel. In promotion and recruitment, emphasis is to be placed on finding those with the relevant training. Secondly, those already in a post, who are not too close to retirement age nor considered to be too politically unsound, will undergo retraining. Finally, education in the Party's organizational principles, its policies and general theoretical education will be stepped up.

The People's Liberation Army, parts of which have provided a source of opposition to the new policies, and its Air Force branch have also declared their intention to upgrade the quality of their cadre force. By 1985 cadres at and below regimental level in the Gansu Military District are to have attained junior secondary school level of education. By 1990, all cadres are to have attained at least the educational level of senior secondary school or of a graduate of a secondary technical school.[41] With respect to promotion in the Air Force it has been stated that priority must be given to cadres trained at military academies and 'intellectual cadres' who graduated from college before the Cultural Revolution. It was said that since the beginning of 1979, 745 cadres with college background had been assigned to leading bodies of the Air Force at division and regimental levels.[42]

In the latter part of 1982 attention was given in the Chinese media to retraining schemes. On 3 October 1982 the Central Committee and State Council decided on a training programme for cadres of the Central Party and government organs on a rotational basis. In general, every cadre is temporarily to leave his or her job every three years to study for six months while still receiving wages and any other benefits. This training is to be related to the cadre's job assignment and the cadre is to be examined and evaluated afterwards. On this point the decision emphasizes again the fact that in appointment and promotion 'educational background, academic performance, work experience and job performance' will be taken into account as 'important foundations'. In future all cadres transferred to central Party and government organs will be expected to have at least an educational and vocational level of senior-middle school or senior technical school. Incumbent cadres under forty years of age with an educational level below that of a junior-middle school graduate are expected to raise their educational level to above junior-middle school within two or three years. Those cadres with an educational level above junior-middle school and without specialized knowledge will be expected to raise their

educational level to that of secondary technical school or
college in three to five years. Conversely, young cadres
with college education but without work experience in basic
units are to be given a chance to 'gain experience in
practical work at the front line'.[43]

In October, 1982 it was announced that the Beijing muni-
cipality had opened its first special course intended
mainly for cadres in their mid-thirties with high-school
education.[44] However, general training programmes have been
under way for some time before these announcements were made.
Since the beginning of 1980, 200,000 cadres above the county
level have received training. This was said to represent
fifty per cent of the total cadre force above the county
level. During the same period, 8,100 Party schools and professional training schools have been reopened or established.
In addition, over 130 institutions of higher learning have
offered professional training courses for 'emerging Party
leaders'. This programme has produced some results. Sixty-
two per cent of directors and vice-directors of the economic
commissions of various provinces and sixty-four per cent of
leading cadres of enterprises above the county level are
said to have received training in enterprise management. In
the agricultural sector, some 62,000 'leading cadres' are
said to have received some kind of training. Finally, Party
secretaries and county heads in over 2,000 counties are said
to have completed their training programme.[45]

Although the thrust of current policy has brought economic
concerns to the forefront, ideological work in general, and
for cadres in particular, has not been forgotten. However,
ideological work and political work are clearly designed to
produce support for the new policies. Towards the end of
1982, Song Renqiong stressed that professional expertise
alone was not enough but must be combined with ideological
and political work. He claimed that this work too was a kind
of science; a 'science for running the Party and the State'.
The implementation of current policy, he wrote, depends on
ideological and political work publicizing and explaining the
policy.[46] Clearly, this work is directed towards eradicating
the continuing opposition to the policies adopted since the
Third Plenum and also towards clearing up the confusion which
must exist in the minds of many cadres given the changes in
Party policy over the last twenty or so years. The problem
of cadre opposition to policy implementation is identified in
the Chinese media by the word factionalism. Despite the
emphasis on the need for greater democracy as a prerequisite
for the four modernizations, three groups of cadres have been
identified to which this advantage will not be extended.
They are: first, followers of the 'Gang of Four'; secondly,
those who have sought to cling too tightly to Mao's legacy;

and thirdly, those who are said to exceed the degree of freedom permissible and who have been denounced as 'anarchists'
or 'bourgeois liberals'. In addition, many cadres are said
not to know how they should behave and how Party and State
should be run. Even among Party members this problem is said
to be particularly acute. The influx of new Party members
during the years 1966-76 is seen as the major cause of this
problem. An article in *Red Flag* estimates that the Party
ranks doubled during this period. As this period is considered a time of 'abnormality' in Party life, many of these
recent recruits are said to be unfamiliar with 'correct
procedures' and hence unqualified to be Party members.[47]
The spectre of a wholesale purge of these people has been
held off and instead an education and rectification programme
is under way for all Party members. In the second half of
1983, a three-year Party rectification programme is to begin
at the end of which all Party members will be required to re-
register. Anyone not reaching the desired standard will be
expelled from the Party or asked to withdraw.[48]

The final set of problems is by no means unique to the
Chinese system but is found in greater or lesser degrees in
all bureaucracies. These concern those who abuse their
position to press their own advantage or in Chinese parlance
those who have transformed themselves from 'public servants
of the people' into 'masters of society'. Harding suggests
that corruption occurs under two sets of circumstances.
First, when the opportunity is present and secondly, when
motivation to be corrupt is high.[49] With respect to the
latter Harding suggests that this might be when officials
are not paid enough. We might add that it can occur when
morale is so low that instead of selflessly dedicating themselves to the collective, cadres dedicate themselves to their
own interests and those of their family. Certainly, in the
post-Mao period, a case can be made for both causes. The
current policies of 'economic liberalization' and the consequent increased contact with other countries have increased
the cadre's opportunity for corruption. The continual
criticism of poor cadre performance, the changing political
lines which often leave cadres exposed to criticism and the
feeling that their positions might cause them to 'miss out'
on some of the advantages of current policy have conspired
to lower cadre morale. These factors combined with the fact
that, initially, there was no effective way to punish errant
cadres, served to compound the problem. The abolition of
'lifetime tenure', the creation of monitoring bodies and
rules and regulations and an increased will to punish
offenders have provided some ability to check the problem.

Nepotism is highlighted as a major problem and cadres
have been criticized for securing the best jobs for their

children and relatives, arranging trips abroad for them and
shielding them from the law if they have committed a crime.
    Initial attempts to resolve these problems were not en-
couraging. Despite the emphasis on the equality of all before the law, the exposés of malpractice tended to concentrate on the lower and middle ranks of the bureaucracy.
Those at the higher levels, and with even greater opportunity to engage in corrupt practices, remained untouched.
Where criticism did touch on higher levels Kraus has shown
that this criticism could be linked to broader political
objectives of the leadership. For example, the criticisms
of Wang Dongxing in the 'unofficial media' for his house-
building exploits can be linked to the attempts to oust him
from the Politburo. The criticisms of Dazhai and Chen
Yonggui can be linked to the attempts to discredit the
agricultural model.[50]
    However, there is evidence of a more genuine and concerted
effort now taking place. Since March 1982, sterner measures
have been introduced to combat corruption. As from March,
corrupt cadres were given the choice of 'owning up now' to
their crimes and receiving seven years' imprisonment or
waiting to be found out and then being taken out and shot![51]
More concerted attempts, it seems, are being made to stop
the children of highly-placed cadres from flouting the law.
It was reported in Hong Kong that Zhao Ziyang, Peng Chong and
Zhang Caiqian each had a son arrested. The sons of the
latter two were said to have been 'running wild in Nanjing
and Shanghai' and to have committed 'countless crimes'.[52]
    The increased number of laws now promulgated, such as the
Code of Criminal Law and the Law of Criminal Procedure, and
the revival of bodies such as the People's Procuratorate can,
if the will is present, provide a sounder basis for prose-
cuting errant cadres. Greater use is being made of formal
and informal mechanisms for monitoring the behaviour of
cadres. For example, one of the tasks of the Commissions for
Inspecting Discipline is to monitor the abuse of privilege
while the increased role of elections in Chinese society and
the abolition of lifelong tenure are both seen as potential
checks on corrupt behaviour. Obviously corruption will not
be eradicated but these appear to be serious attempts to
bring it under control.

CONCLUDING REMARKS

The extent to which these reforms have been and are likely to
prove successful is mixed. Leaving aside the question of
whether or not there may be another change in political line

in China there are still problems to be faced even if the present policies are continued.

In April 1982, Zhao Ziyang reported on the progress of the administrative reforms. The number of ministries and commissions was reduced from fifty-two to forty-one. On the basis of statistics from thirty-eight of these, the reduction in the number of personnel has been impressive. A total of 505 ministers and vice-ministers was cut to 167, and the average age was reduced from sixty-four to fifty-eight. Similar reductions were made at the department and bureau level. Based on the data from twenty-eight ministries and commissions, the number of department and bureau heads has been reduced from 2,450 to 1,398 with a drop in average age from fifty-nine to fifty-four.[53] Similar reforms in the Party apparatus have also been taking place. In May 1982, changes at the department level of the Party were announced. The number of heads and deputy heads was reduced by 15.7 per cent, and the average age from sixty-four to sixty. The total staff of the thirty departments under the Central Committee is said to have been reduced by 17.3 per cent.[54]

A more severe test of these reforms will come when the programme is extended to the provincial level during 1983 and when it is subsequently extended to the basic levels. If the reforms do not penetrate properly through the middle to the lower levels of the bureaucracy then the reform efforts of those at the top will have been in vain. Even at the higher levels problems remain. For the programme to be truly effective, retirement must become institutionalized and thus become a natural part of the work-cycle. If the current reforms prove to be no more than a 'one-off event' then within a few years the figures for average ages will creep back up and the system will once again become clogged with geriatrics.

The creation of advisory positions has meant that many of those 'retiring' have simply moved to newly-created posts. Although the advisory commission to the Central Committee, for example, is referred to as a temporary phenomenon brought about by the particular circumstances of the time, it remains to be seen whether, having been conjured up as a temporary expedient, it will prove as easy to be spirited away. It is difficult to see what the real change would be if, for example, all the oldest Party cadres simply became advisers. With respect to the Party the immediate effect of creating advisory commissions has been to increase the number of people attending plenary sessions of the Central Committee. The Seventh Plenum of the Eleventh Central Committee (August 1982) was attended by a total of 318 people (297 Committee members and alternates and twenty-one observers) while the first Plenum of the Twelfth Central Committee was

attended by 631 people (347 Committee members and alternates
and 284 observers). This 100 per cent increase does not bode
well for a regime committed to reducing bureaucracy. Clearly,
this system cannot serve as a long-term solution, and an
effective retirement system must be institutionalized.

Even if this problem is resolved the even greater problems
of training, recruiting and promoting skilled personnel will
remain. Progress with this has been made at the higher levels
but again the real test rests with getting better qualified
people into the cadre force at the basic levels. The reforms
of the State structure have increased the number of college-
educated ministers and vice-ministers from thirty-seven to
fifty-two per cent of the total. Based on data from twenty-
eight of the ministries and commissions, the percentage of
college-educated department and bureau heads is said to have
increased from thirty-six to forty-nine per cent.[55] The percentage of specialized personnel on the Central Committee is
said to have increased from 2.7 per cent on the Eleventh to
seventeen per cent on the Twelfth Central Committee.[56] While
this represents impressive increases it will become increasingly difficult to keep raising them further. The
current percentages of educated personnel still fall far
short of what one would expect of officials in such positions.
Also, evidence supports that there is continued opposition to
these policies.

The crucial problem, however, remains whether the educational system can be expanded rapidly enough to train
sufficient quantities of people to the required levels in a
short enough time. Although this is recognized as a major
problem hindering progress it seems unlikely that sufficient
money and resources can be found. Deng Xiaoping highlighted
this problem in his January Report and stated that it was
'absolutely imperative' for spending on education, science,
culture and public health to be increased, otherwise modernization could not be achieved.[57] Despite increased spending
on education it must still compete with other sectors for
scarce resources. As a consequence the system of 'key
institutions' has been revived. The institutions receive
preferential treatment in terms of investment, allocation of
teachers and selection of students and are expected to produce the best results. It is seen as a way of maximizing
returns on limited investments. To back up the policies the
vocational and technical secondary schools have been revived
and greater use is being made of correspondence courses and
the Television University. It is hoped that the latter will
produce large returns for little input. However, this is
unlikely to produce a sufficient number of cadres with the
relevant skills to replace the incumbent cadre corps quickly

enough. Clearly on-the-job retraining will have to play an
important role.

People must also be sufficiently motivated to become cadres
and take on the extra responsibilities and risks involved.
Despite the measures to upgrade the status of intellectuals,
many intellectuals must still be suspicious of putting themselves in a position where they could be exposed to criticism
at a later date. In the countryside evidence exists to
suggest that people are becoming less willing to join the
Party. If the current policies mean that the privileged
access to goods that Party membership gives is undermined and
rivalled by other avenues for accumulating them, people may
decide that the gains of being a Party member, and in particular a cadre, do not outweigh the gains that can be made elsewhere. Also, peasants and workers may feel that the stress on
the exemplary behaviour that cadres should display could prevent them from taking full advantage of current policies.

Although the current leadership has the desire to change
the structure of its cadre force it will be no easy matter to
replace the veteran general administrative cadres by younger
cadres with specific expertise. Ironically, the current
leadership might find it easier to secure the 'political
integrity' part of their equation rather than the 'professional
competence' part. It may prove easier to recruit and re-
educate a cadre force dedicated to the implementation of the
policies adopted since the Third Plenum. Given the problems
discussed above it might not prove so easy to ensure that the
cadre force, particularly those at the basic levels, will
possess the necessary skills to create and manage a modern
economy.

NOTES

1.   Essentially, a cadre is any person who holds a formal
        leadership post at any level in any organization. The
        cadre is the key component in the Chinese system, pro-
        viding the backbone of policy implementation. One might
        refer to a military cadre or a Party cadre depending on
        the organization in which they work, or to a basic-
        level or high-level cadre depending on their respective
        position within the hierarchy of that organization. The
        cadre need not necessarily be a Communist Party member
        but he or she will be expected to provide good leader-
        ship for the masses, listen to their views and, at the
        same time, remain responsive to policy directives from
        above. Depending on the organization in which they work
        cadres have a different system of salary classification

and grades. For more details see Doak Barnett, 1967, 34ff and *passim*.

2. Mao Zedong, 1938.
'The Role of the Chinese Communist Party in the National War'. In *Selected Works of Mao Tse-tung*, Vol. 2. Beijing: Foreign Languages Press, 1965, p. 202.

3. Vogel, E.F., 1974.
'Politicised Bureaucracy: Communist China'. In *Communist Systems in Comparative Perspective* (eds.) L.J. Cohe and J.P. Shapiro. New York: Anchor Books, p. 165.

4. Kautsky, J., 1971.
The Political Consequences of Modernisation. New York: John Wiley and Sons, passim.

5. Party Constitution, 1982.
Adopted by the Twelfth National Congress of the Communist Party of China. In *Beijing Review*, No. 38, p. 11.

6. People's Daily Commentator, 1978. 'Consolidation Means Revolution'. In *People's Daily*, 3 June.

7. Hu Yaobang, 1980.
Interview with Tanjug, Correspondent, in *Summary of World Broadcasts: the Far East*, 6453.

8. Hua Guofeng, 1979.
'Report on the Work of the Government'. In *Main Documents of the Second Session of the Fifth National People's Congress of the People's Republic of China*. Beijing: Foreign Languages Press, pp. 72-3.

9. Ibid, pp. 48-9.

10. Ye Jianying, 1979.
'Speech in Commemoration of the Thirtieth Anniversary of the People's Republic of China'. In *Beijing Review*, No. 40, pp. 27-30.

11. Ibid, p. 28.

12. Ibid.

13. People's Daily Commentator, 1979.
'Strict Demands Must Be Made on Leading Cadres'. In *People's Daily*, 28 October.

14. *Red Flag,* No. 16, 1980.

15. Deng Xiaoping, 1980b.
    'Speech at an Enlarged Meeting of the Politbureau',
    August 1980. In *Issues and Studies,* Vol. XVII, No. 3,
    1981, 78-103, p. 83.

16. Ibid. p. 93.

17. Deng Xiaoping, 1980a.
    'Sixteenth January Report of the Current Situation and
    Tasks'. In *Summary of World Broadcasts: the Far East,*
    6363.

18. Song Renqiong, 1980.
    'Concerning several Questions of the Future Origin of
    Cadres not Engaged in Production'. In *People's Daily,*
    9 July.

19. People's Daily Special Commentator, 1980.
    'On Correctly Comprehending the Problem of Paying
    Attention to Culture When Selecting Cadres'. In
    People's Daily, 16 December.

20. Hua Guofeng, 1980.
    'Speech at the Third Session of the Fifth National
    People's Congress'. In *Main Documents of the Third
    Session of the Fifth National People's Congress of the
    People's Republic of China.* Beijing: Foreign Languages
    Press.

21. Red Flag Commentator, 1981.
    'Several Questions Concerning the Strengthening of
    Party Leadership'. In *Red Flag,* No. 2.

22. See for example *Summary of World Broadcasts: the Far
    East* (SWB:FE), 1982, 7125.

23. Harding, H. 1981.
    Organising China. Stanford: Stanford University Press,
    p. 294.

24. Peng Xiangfu and Zheng Zhangbing, 1980.
    'A Talk on Abolishing the System of Lifetime Tenure for
    Cadres'. In *People's Daily,* 3 June.

25. People's Daily Commentator, 1980.
    'An Important Reform of the Leadership System of the
    Party and State'. In *People's Daily,* 28 October.

26. Deng Xiaoping, 1980a, cf. note 17.

27. February 1980.

28. Draft Party Constitution.
     In *Issues and Studies,* Vol. XVI, No. 9, 81-109,
     p. 103.

29. Hu Qiaomu, 1982.
     'Some Questions Concerning Revision of the Party
     Constitution'. In *Beijing Review,* No. 39.

30. Song Renqiong, 1982.
     'Build a Good Cadre Contingent According to the
     Principle that They Must be More Revolutionary, Younger
     in Average Age, More Educated and Professionally More
     Competent'. In *People's Daily,* 2 October.

31. Red Flag Commentator, 1980.
     'Be Promotors in Reforming the Structure of Cadre
     Ranks'. In *Red Flag* No. 11.

32. People's Daily Editorial, 1982.
     'Why Is It Said that the Current Historical Period Is
     One of the Best Since the Founding of the People's
     Republic of China: Supporting Evidence in Ten Fields'.
     In *People's Daily,* 29 October.

33. People's Daily Commentator, 1982.
     'The Glorious and Sacred Obligation of Veteran Cadres'.
     In *People's Daily,* 3 March.

34. Song Renqiong, 1982.
     'Educate Party Members in the New Party Constitution,
     Make Ideological Reparations for Party Rectification'.
     In *Red Flag* No. 24.

35. An article in the Hong Kong paper *Ming Pao* reporting
     the Central Committee document stated that ministers
     would be expected to retire at sixty-five. Cadres at
     or below the levels of vice-minister, directors of
     departments and bureaux, directors of divisions and
     directors of sections would be expected to retire at
     sixty. The article also reported that a retirement age
     of eighty was being considered for 'leaders of Party
     and State'. (In SWB:FE, 1982, 6969).

36. In SWB:FE, 1982, 6969.

37.   Anhui Provincial CCP Committee Organization Department
      1980.
      'Train a Great Contingent of Red and Expert Cadres'.   In
      Red Flag, No. 4.

38.   Cf. note 32.

39.   See for example Song Dahan and Zhang Chunsheng, 1982.
      'Important Change in the System of People's Communes'.
      In *Beijing Review*, No. 29.

40.   Qin Li, 1982.
      'What a Theoretical Test Shows'.   In *Red Flag*, No. 9.

41.   SWB:FE, 1982, 7197.

42.   SWB:FE, 1982, 7146.

43.   SWB:FE, 1982, 7158.

44.   SWB:FE, 1982, 7146.

45.   SWB:FE, 1982, 7157.

46.   Song Renqiong, *Red Flag*, 1982, cf. Note 34.

47.   Zhang Yun, 1980.
      'Enhance Party Spirit, Strive for a Fundamental Turn in
      Party Workstyle'.   In *Red Flag*, No. 3.

48.   Hu Yaobang, 1982.
      'Create a New Situation in All Fields of Socialism and
      Modernisation'.   In *Beijing Review*, No. 37, p. 38.

49.   Harding, op. cit. pp. 7-8.

50.   Kraus, R., 1983.
      'Bureaucratic Privilege as an Issue in Chinese
      Politics'.   In *World Development*, August, 1983,
      pp. 673-82.

51.   *Manchester Guardian*, 16 March, 1982.

52.   Pai Hsing, 1 October 1982 reported in SWB:FE 1982,
      7149.

53.   SWB:FE, 1982, 7014.

54.   SWB:FE, 1982, 7028.

55.   SWB:FE, 1982, 7014.

56.   SWB:FE, 1982, 7129.

57.   Deng Xiaoping, 1980a, cf. note 17.

REFERENCES

Anhui Provincial CCP Committee Organization Department, 1980.
'Train a Great Contingent of Red and Expert Cadres'.   In
Red Flag, No. 4.

Beijing Review, 1979.   'Lessons from a Case of Embezzlement'.
In *Beijing Review,* No. 20.

Beijing Review, 1983.   'Young Cadres Raised to Leading Posts'.
In *Beijing Review,* No. 1.

Deng Xiaoping, 1980a.   'Sixteenth January Report on the Current
Situation and Tasks'.   In *Summary of World Broadcasts:
the Far East,* 6363.

Deng Xiaoping, 1980b.   'Speech at an Enlarged Meeting of the
Politburo, August 1980'.   In *Issues and Studies,*
vol. XVII, No. 3, 1981, 78-103.

'Draft Party Constitution'.   In *Issues and Studies,* vol. XVI,
No. 9, 81-109.

Harding, H. 1981. *Organizing China.*   Stanford: Stanford Univ.
Press.

Hu Qiaomu, 1982.   'Some Questions Concerning Revision of the
Party Constitution'.   In *Beijing Review,* No. 39.

Hu Yaobang, 1980.   'Interview with Tanjug Correspondent'.
In *Summary of World Broadcasts: the Far East,* 6453.

Hu Yaobang, 1982.   'Create a New Situation in All Fields of
Socialism and Modernization'.   In *Beijing Review,* No. 37.

Hua Guofeng, 1979.   'Report on the Work of the Government'.
In *Main Documents of the Second Session of the Fifth
National People's Congress of the People's Republic
of China.*   Beijing: Foreign Languages Press.

Hua Guofeng, 1980. 'Speech at the Third Session of the Fifth National People's Congress'. In *Main Documents of the Third Session of the Fifth National People's Congress of the People's Republic of China*. Beijing: Foreign Languages Press.

Kautsky J., 1971. *'The Political Consequences of Modernization*. New York: John Wiley and Sons.

Kraus R., 1982. 'The Pacification of Class Conflict'. Paper delivered to the China in transition Conference, Queen Elizabeth House, Oxford, 7-10 September 1982.

Mao Zedong, 1938. 'The Role of the Chinese Communist Party in the National War'. In *Selected Works of Mao Tse-tung*, vol. 2. Beijing: Foreign Languages Press, 1965.

Party Constitution, 1982. Adopted by the Twelfth National Congress of the Communist Party of China. In *Beijing Review*, No. 38.

Peng Xiangfu and Zheng Zhangbing, 1980. 'A Talk on Abolishing the System of Lifetime Tenure for Cadres'. In *People's Daily*, 3 June.

People's Daily Commentator, 1978. 'Consolidation Means Revolution'. In *People's Daily*, 20 March.

People's Daily Commentator, 1979. 'Strict Demands Must Be Made on Leading Cadres'. In *People's Daily*, 15 August.

People's Daily Commentator, 1980. 'An Important Reform of the Leadership System of the Party and State'. In *People's Daily*, 28 October.

People's Daily Commentator, 1982. 'The Glorious and Sacred Obligation of Veteran Cadres'.In *People's Daily*, 3 March.

People's Daily Editorial, 1982. 'Why is it Said that the Current Historical Period is One of the Best Since the Founding of the People's Republic of China? Supporting Evidence in Ten Fields'. In *People's Daily*, 29 October.

People's Daily Special Commentator, 1980. 'On Correctly Comprehending the Problem of Paying Attention to Culture When Selecting Cadres'. In *People's Daily*, 16 December.

Qin Li, 1982. 'What a Theoretical Test Shows'. In *Red Flag*, No. 9.

Red Flag Commentator, 1980. 'Be Promotors in Reforming the Structure of Cadre Ranks'. In *Red Flag,* No. 11.

Red Flag Commentator, 1981. 'Several Questions Concerning the Strengthening of Party Leadership'. In *Red Flag,* No. 2.

Song Dahan and Zhang Chunsheng, 1982. 'Important Change in the System of People's Communes'. In *Beijing Review,* No. 29.

Song Renqiong, 1980. 'Concerning Several Questions of the Future Origin of Cadres not Engaged in Production'. In *People's Daily,* 9 July.

Song Renqiong, 1982. 'Build a Good Cadre Contingent According to the Principle that they must be More Revolutionary, Younger in Average Age, More Educated and Professionally More Competent'. In *People's Daily,* 2 October.

Song Renqiong, 1982. 'Educate Party Members in the New Party Constitution, Make Ideological Reparations for Party Rectification'. In *Red Flag,* No. 24.

Vogel, E.F., 1974. 'Politicized Bureaucracy: Communist China'. In *Communist Systems in Comparative Perspective* (eds.) L.J. Cohen and J.P. Shapiro. New York: Anchor Books.

Wang Renzhong, 1982. 'Unify Thinking, Conscientiously Rectify Workstyle'. In *Red Flag,* No. 5.

Ye Jianying, 1979. 'Speech in Commemoration of the Thirtieth Anniversary of the People's Republic of China'. In *Beijing Review,* No. 40.

Zhang Yun, 1980. 'Enhance Party Spirit, Strive for a Fundamental Turn in Party Workstyle'. In *Red Flag,*No. 3.

Zheng Feng, 1982. 'How Can There By Any Talk of Flexibility in Party Workstyle'.*Nanfang Ribao,* 12 February. In *Summary of World Broadcasts: the Far East,* 6965.

6

AGRICULTURE AND ECOLOGY IN CHINA

E.B. Vermeer

Editors' Introduction

Chinese agriculture is now facing serious limitations of natural resources. One-third of the total farmland is marginal, low-yield land. To develop it into high-quality land, huge investments would be needed. E.B. Vermeer in the present paper raises the question as to whether marginal land should continue to produce foodgrain or any crop at all. Focusing on the ecological problems imposed by salinization, soil erosion, decreasing water resources, and deforestation, the author discusses the Chinese agricultural development issues, their background, and the possible implications.

Most parts of China's 9.6 million square kilometres are of little or no use to man. Extreme coldness or high altitude (such as on the Qinghai-Tibet plateau), extreme dryness (such as in the deserts of Xinjiang and inner Mongolia) and steepness of slopes are major factors limiting habitation or agriculture. According to present statistics, the cultivated area is 100 million ha, or only 10 per cent or so of China's total land surface.[1] However, as with most statistics on China, this figure is dubious. Local surveys have shown that there are around 120 million ha.

The Chinese themselves have expressed similar doubts concerning the official figure for China's forest area reporting that there are approximately 122 million ha, representing 13 per cent of China's total land surface. In reality, satellite pictures show that China's forest cover is only about half that size, 5 per cent according to some, 8 per cent according to others.[2] Obviously, a matter of definition is involved. At present, we have little choice but to follow the Chinese official figures, but with reservations.

While the rural population doubled between 1949 and 1980, from 425 million to more than 800 million,[3] the size of total farmland area has remained surprisingly stable. However, its composition changed a great deal. Much prime land was taken up by State capital construction projects, rural housing, land improvement measures and roads. Some farmland was converted into grassland or became wasteland. Altogether the farmland area may have been reduced by 30 million ha since 1949.[4] Almost the same amount of new farmland was created by reclamation during this period.[5] Most of this land, however, is not very productive because of unfavourable natural conditions.[6] Thus the quality of China's farmland has changed considerably over the past 30 years: marginal areas which are saline or marshy or sandy or subject to serious erosion etc., now constitute about one-third of the total farmland area, with average grain yields below 1.1 ton per ha.[7] Likewise, about one-third of the farmland area (probably for a large part overlapping with the marginal one-third) was struck by disaster each year from 1972 to 1977, a considerably larger area than during the 1950s.[8] On the other hand, there is about one-third of the total farmland which has been much improved by infrastructural measures such as pump irrigation and drainage, land levelling, mechanical ploughing and high levels of chemical fertilizer application. This one-third is responsible for two-thirds of China's grain production and for almost all of its cotton.[9] Agricultural modernization has widened the differentials between low- and high-production areas[10] to such an extent that the question has arisen *'Should marginal areas continue to be used for the cultivation of foodgrain or any crop at all?*

As is well known, most peasants down through history have answered this question with their feet, by moving elsewhere when no satisfactory income could be derived from agriculture in marginal areas. However, the Chinese case is different for two reasons. One is that already before China became industrialized, all easily accessible and promising land had been opened up for cultivation under the heavy pressure of population increase. The other is that since the formation of the People's Communes in 1958 the members of the production teams have been tied to the soil of their native villages and not allowed to move. This limitation of the peasants' mobility has served to keep the city population down to the very low levels of 99 million in 1957, 102 million in 1970, and 129 million in 1980.[11] By 1978 industrial employment, inclusive of industries operated by People's Communes, was no larger than 50 million, as against 295 million agricultural labourers,[12] so almost all rural population growth has been accommodated within the villages.

Furthermore, during the past 30 years, a considerable amount of capital has been invested in the development of agriculture, both by the State and by the local communities: 120 billion *yuan* in water conservancy and irrigation, 110 billion *yuan* by the State alone in agriculture, and a difficult-to-assess amount in tractors, chemical fertilizer industry, etc.[13] According to a recent estimate, agricultural modernization (along the lines previously suggested by Hua Guofeng's 1978-85 Plan) would require a tremendous amount of capital: for an average count of half a million people about 200 million *yuan*.[14] Thus, for China as a whole this might

take 300 billion *yuan* - three times the *total* annual State
budget which is clearly unrealistic at this time. As it is,
most of China's marginal and poor agricultural areas will
have to do without much State investment in the near future.
So the question poses itself again: should marginal areas continue to be used for cultivation of foodgrain or for any
crop at all? This question has several angles: a production
angle, a productivity angle, an employment angle, a capital
requirement angle, and last but not least the ecological and
long-term conservation-of-resources angle. There is no easy
answer, and the question 'if not agriculture, then what?'
must be asked as well. Only very recently has the problem
been recognized as such in China. With accessibility and
official data being what they are, we are in no position to
give more than a preliminary answer for some areas, based on
available literature, satellite pictures and visitors' reports. Satellite pictures are especially useful in identi-
fying natural vegetation and crops, in indicating surface
water resources, in classification of soils, and in expanding
data. They facilitate the drawing of demarcation lines between different crop zones and provide a basis for inter-
regional comparison. In the following, we will discuss six
areas in different parts of China, and then we shall draw
some conclusions concerning agriculture and forestry, and
suggest possible measures to protect the environment.

1. NEW OASES IN XINJIANG AND SECONDARY SALINIZATION

The arid North-west of China used to be inhabited by nomads
who tended their cattle on the mountain slopes and desert
fringes. Generally, precipitation in the area is only 50-
100 mm a year and evaporation about 2,000 mm; therefore, only
in some areas with access to water from mountain streams or
from underground water resources is agriculture possible and
feasible. Since 1949 the reclamation corps of the People's
Liberation Army has undertaken a major effort in reclamation
and grain production, against very adverse natural conditions.
Soils are sandy and irrigation water seeps away quickly;
strong winds in spring and heat in summer cause high evaporation; the few rivers have a very irregular regime. All these
factors contribute to ready alkalization of the soil.[15] The
oases in the Tarim river area (the northern fringe of the
Taklamakan desert) have a history of agriculture dating back
to the Han dynasty, but they never seemed very promising.
Still, Chinese authorities find 262,000 ha along the Tarim
River lower reaches suitable for reclamation.[16]

Since 1949, the old irrigation areas were expanded, and new
State Farms were built. In the past 20 years and more, over

70,000 ha were reclaimed, and new oases were created. With
the increase of the irrigated area, the water of the Tarim
river dwindled, and the quality of lake, reservoir and river
water deteriorated. In the non-reclaimed grasslands near the
river the water-table dropped, the plant cover declined from
10 to 15 per cent in the past to 2 to 4 per cent now, and
grass stands became very poor, going down from 1200-2250
kg/ha to 270-375 kg/ha. The forest cover in the upper reaches
decreased to one-third of what it was before reclamation.
Consequently, the ecological balance was seriously disturbed.

Along the Tarim river, total dissolved salts did not constitute more than one per cent of total water weight in the
late 1950s and early 1960s. Up to the mid-seventies, salinity
increased by 5-8 times during the spring flow (April-June).
After 15 years of cultivation it appeared that ground water in
the belt with a width of about 10 km along the Tarim River rose
from 4-6 m below the surface (3-8 m in the lower reaches) to
1-3 m below the surface. Salinity rose from the original
1-3 g/l to 3-10 g/l. Ground water rose because of irrigation
without sufficient drainage. Thereby, salts were brought up to
the crop root zone. Commenting on these facts, a Chinese
author concluded that: (A) irrigation water should be used in a
more rational and sparing way; (B) drainage should be improved;
(C) forests and pastures should be protected.[17]

Indeed the salt levels threaten the very survival of these
oases. Moreover, the desiccation of the pastures will take
away the livelihood of the native nomad population and bring
the desert and sand storms down to the agricultural fields.
From a purely economic point of view, only high-quality cotton
seems a rewarding staple crop (as it is capable of resisting
fairly high levels of salinity). Also, the strategic need to
establish a Han-Chinese presence and a food base for the PLA is
not as valid a legitimation for maintaining agricultural production in this interior area as it is for the Northern
Xinjiang border. So there seem to be many good reasons for
reducing the area for agriculture.

2. THE LOESS PLATEAU AND WATER AND SOIL EROSION

How to manage the serious water and soil erosion problems of
the 580,000 sq km loess plateau in Gansu, Shaanxi and Shanxi
Provinces has been the subject of a continuous debate during
this century. The focus was mainly on the reduction of the
extremely heavy silt load of the Yellow River, which created
problems for containment of the river in the North China
Plain, and for the construction of reservoirs.[18] Later it
seems that the inevitability of a high silt content was recognized and more attention was given to the economic and eco-

logical problems of the loess plateau itself. The population
in the area had increased to 60 million by 1980[19] and nowadays
the area is extremely poor.[20] Northern Shaanxi was once rich
in water and natural vegetation. At the end of the fifteenth
century, reclamation started and grain was sown. After five
centuries of cultivation, most of the area is now a semi-
desert and suffers from droughts and sandstorms. For every
hectare of land taken into cultivation, three hectares of
grassland are turned into desert, and after 1949 there has
been no management of pastures. As people only wanted products - meat, wool and hides - the best pastureland was put to
the plough, and of the remaining pastures, over-grazing became
an increasing problem.[21]

Guyan County in Gansu has been publicized as a case in
point. It is a mountainous, dry and seriously eroded area. It
should have been devoted to animal husbandry, but since 1949
grain production was developed instead. Between 1949 and 1979
the population increased by 133 per cent; 82,000 ha were reclaimed, so that the cultivated area rose from 203,000 ha to
285,000 ha or 0.57 ha per person by 1980. Average foodgrain
yield, however, was only 315 kg per ha, so that per capita
grain production in 1978 was less than half the amount in
1949, viz. 178 kg in 1978 as against 414 kg 3 decades earlier.
The quantities of pork, meat and edible oil sold to the State
declined greatly, and the area has been dependent on State
relief during the 1970s.[22]

Chinese plans for the loess area economy stress the development of animal husbandry and forestry, and reduction of the
foodgrain acreage. This is a realistic option only if a long-
term commitment is made to provide the area with extra foodgrain during years of drought (such as happened in 1980). To
that end it is also imperative that communications and transport facilities are improved, in order to be able to move
grain in and meat, wool, fruit and other products out to
Xi'an, Lanzhou, Baotou and other cities. The promotion of
green manure has already shown favourable effects, and provincial authorities urge peasants to sow green fertilizer
crops immediately after the wheat harvest or autumn harvest to
improve soil structure and fertility, (and to provide fodder
for pigs). In irrigated areas *chengma* (latin name: caetalaria
juncea) is also important, in dry areas green beans and blade
beans. One might also try an 'unpopular' crop such as Irish
potatoes, and promote other economic activities such as coal
mining. These suggestions were made by provincial authorities
to the author of this article during a visit to Shaanxi
Province in 1979. The felt potatoes seem to be a good idea
(climate and soil being suitable), but growing this crop would
need considerable pushing, as the peasants are not accustomed
to eating these potatoes. Moreover, Irish potatoes still

count as a vegetable crop, and not as food grain crop. This
has implications for fixing official targets for foodgrain
production. Developing coal mining would need considerable
investments and improvement of existing railways. Local
officials are in favour of it, but they are not very optimistic about prospects for getting the necessary funds. Finally,
the drawing of underground water from depths of over 70-100
metres for irrigation purposes seems uneconomical considering
the rising energy prices. Consequently, agriculture does not
seem to have much of a future in this area. If the government
would want a major reforestation effort at the middle reaches
of the Huanghe to support agriculture downstream, it should
then subsidize the local peasants for carrying it out, or move
in labourers from outside. The latter should not be necessary
as the area is clearly overpopulated; to do so would cause
serious unemployment. However, nature seems to be stronger
than man in this area. It is doubtful whether large-scale
afforestation is possible under the dry climatic conditions
which characterized the seventies, and whether continuing process of erosion can be slowed down.

3. THE SANJIANG PLAIN AND THE DRYING UP
OF MARSHES AND PASTURES

Only very recently an article in *Dili Xuebao* drew attention to
the reclamation of marshland area in the extreme North-east of
China.[23] The Sanjiang ('Three rivers') plain, at the confluence of the Heilong river and the Wusuli river, is an
alluvial marshland with a surface of 51,300 sq km. During the
early fifties about 25 per cent of the area was marshland, 30
per cent was fluctuating between marshland and grassland, over
30 per cent grassland, 8 per cent forest and 3 per cent water-
bodies. Formerly, in the marshes there were many small lakes.
The forest area mostly consisted of shrubs, where wildlife was
abundant with bears, deer, otters, foxes and fish. Now wildlife has been much reduced as it was dependent on a marshy
environment.

In 1949, only 3 per cent of the area was farmland; but by
1979 this had been expanded to 36 per cent of the total area,
i.e. to 1,800,000 ha, and it has been estimated that a further
2,900,000 ha of wasteland is reclaimable.[24] Being located
in a strategic position on the Soviet border, it has become
one of China's granaries selling more than half of its grain
production to the State.

But there was no unified reclamation plan. North of the
Sungari, 30,000 ha of reclaimed sandy soil turned into a sand
desert. The forests were almost entirely destroyed and merely
covered 5 per cent of the area in 1974. Marshes then covered

1,160,000 ha, fluctuating marsh/grassland 1,120,000 ha; altogether the marshes covered 47 per cent of the total area. During the past few years this marsh/grassland area decreased by a further 53,000 ha per year. Thus animal life changed considerably. Fish production in 1979 was only 17 per cent of that in 1960.

The average amount of rainfall decreased from 600-700 mm in the early 1950s to 400-450 mm in the second half of the 1970s.[25] Surface water flow decreased, and the water-table fell. Wind and sand affected soil fertility, contributing to desertification. Salinization affected over 60,000 ha, and water and soil erosion became more serious. Thus, agriculture suffered as well.

The author of the article in *Dili Xuebao* proposed several measures to be taken for rational use of natural resources:

(a)   Protective forests should be planted. Forest renewal must be stimulated. Animal husbandry and fisheries should be developed.
      Agricultural areas should be limited to 45-50 per cent, grassland for animal husbandry to 20 per cent, forest cover should be 10-15 per cent, area for sideline production and protected marshes 10-15 per cent, waterbodies 3 per cent.

(b)   Water management should be comprehensive. Underground water must be used. The region has experience with rice (85,000 ha in 1980), and more rice should be planted because it is highly productive and helps maintain the ecological system.

(c)   Soil should be nourished to raise its fertility. Green fertilizer should be planted, stalks and ashes should be used, and other organic fertilizers.

(d)   A certain area of marshes should be protected as a necessary factor in the ecological balance. These should be designated as such.

In the absence of data on land and water resources in this area, and on economic and demographic developments, it is very hard to comment on these proposals. The picture of ecological losses is much clearer than that of possible economic gains from agriculture or forestry. The development of the area seems to be bound up with the presence of the PLA and its economic demands.

4. TIANJIN WATER SUPPLY

The northernmost part of the North China Plain, with the two large cities of Beijing and Tianjin, has a severe water shortage.[26] Precipitation is only 500 to 550 mm per year, of which three-quarters falls during the summer months of June to September. Tianjin now has a population of nine million. Its water consumption is 65 times as much as that of 1950 because of increases in industry, population and agriculture. Its traditional water source, the Haihe river, has been increasingly tapped upstream for irrigation purposes. Since 1958 over 20 large reservoirs were built on the upper reaches of the Haihe river tributaries, so Tianjin received less and less water. In 1980 only 0.7 billion cubic metres of water entered the sea, or 8.5 per cent of the pre-1958 amount. In the drought year of 1972, when precipitation was only 314 mm, water was let in from the Huanghe via the Grand Canal. In 1975 and again during 1980 and 1981, the water shortage in Tianjin was very serious.

Tianjin's city districts draw more than 0.1 billion cubic metres of underground water per year. But the water-table is steadily falling, so that pumping costs have increased both for city and for agricultural users. There is now an area of 7,000 square kilometres where the water table is 60 metres lower than in the surrounding areas. The surface of Tianjin has sunk by 80 cm during the past 20 years, in one place even by 150 cm.[27]

The surface water is not only getting scarcer, but also dirtier because of factory pollution.[28] The seawater entering the Haihe river makes the water more saline. As a solution, reservoirs have been built on the plains, some very large, but these depend on water from upstream and also tend to become saline.[29] Two reservoirs are under construction as a part of the Luan river control scheme. These will be able to provide urban and rural Tangshan and Tianjin with an estimated two billion cubic metres of water per year. A diversion project which can supply Huanghe river water to Tianjin was completed in 1982.[30] Together they will somewhat ease the present situation which is representative of all East coast cities from Beijing to Shanghai. Especially in the Beijing-Tianjin area the competing demands for water for industrial, urban and agricultural uses face a permanent shortage of surface water, which cannot be made up by underground water any more. Agriculture probably will have to give way.

5. RECLAMATION OF LAKES -
'DRAINING THE POND TO CATCH THE FISH'?

Since 1949, China's lake surface decreased by 1.3 million ha, mostly along the middle reaches of the Yangzi river. The silting up and reclamation of lakes has occurred throughout China's history, but has speeded up considerably after 1949.[31] During the past 30 years, the Dongting Lake has shrunk from 435,000 ha to 282,000 ha.[32] Many smaller lakes in Hubei have been reclaimed,[33] and their total surface has diminished by three-quarters. Of the Poyang Lake in Jiangxi at least 87,000 ha have been reclaimed, or more.[34] The flood danger along the middle reaches of the Yangzi river has considerably increased, because of the loss of flood water storage capacity, a fact which became painfully clear during the 1980 floods.[35]

Generally speaking, the drainage and reclamation of lakes lowers their water retention capacity, so that in dry periods the more elevated surrounding areas no longer have irrigation water from the lake. After heavy rainfall there is bound to be waterlogging, and the costs of pumping water out may be very high. A recent article also pointed to some other negative effects: after reduction of the surface of the Chaohu Lake in Anhui, its influence in prolonging the frostfree period by 20 to 40 days in this area was much weakened, which had bad effects on production. Similarly, a decision to maintain the water level of the Baiyangding Lake (near Baoding, south of Beijing) at 1.7 metres has had a favourable influence on tempering the climate in this region.[36] Of course there are negative effects on fishery as well. Fresh water fish production went down from 500,000 tons during the fifties to 300,000 tons during the seventies.[37] The Taihu lake in Jiangsu, which lost 20,000 ha through reclamation, did not fall off in quantity of fish production, but fewer and fewer large fish were caught, as large fish are more vulnerable to water pollution, and undoubtedly also because of over-fishing.[38]

In spite of these negative effects, it seems that reclamation of lakes in the Yangzi river basin is profitable. The reclaimed land is very productive, and situated in densely-populated areas with good communications. The surrounding fields usually can make up the loss of irrigation water supply by using underground water close to the surface. The loss of fish can be compensated for by meat from animal husbandry. Because of the flood danger, however, more often than not the reclaimed areas might be best devoted to raising cattle so that they can still be used as flood diversion areas whenever necessary. The meat has a ready market in nearby Wuhan and might be exported via the Yangzi river. This should be more

profitable than the alternative of wheat followed by green
fertilizer crops and safer and less costly than full-fledged
farming behind high dikes.

6. HAINAN ISLAND SLASH-AND-BURN

Hainan has a rich variety of plant species, and many very
valuable kinds of timber and medicinal herbs. However,
because of indiscriminate felling of trees since the 1950s,
the ecological balance has been seriously disturbed. The
natural forest decreased from 863,000 ha to 245,000 ha in
1980 - a decrease of 72 per cent. The forest cover decreased
from 25 per cent in 1954 to 13.6 per cent, with an additional
7.8 per cent of rubber trees or protective forests. A
Chinese visitor noted that during 1979-1980 forest destruction
had worsened fast:

> During a cross-country drive this year's April we saw much
> destruction along the road. Although there are many signs
> to protect the forest and forbid fires yet slash-and-burn
> farming continues; burning the mountain slopes to catch
> the 'Money Tortoise' (which is sold at high prices to
> Hongkong merchants) is still on the increase. On the
> mountains everywhere you see smoke, and the traces of de-
> struction by forest fires are a sad sight. The protective
> tree belts along the road have been plundered at many
> places, terrible.[39]

He attributed the forest destruction to four causes: (1) the
policy of 'taking grain as the key link'; (2) primitive
slash-and-burn methods; (3) the expansion of State farms,
from an area of 27,000 ha in 1960 to 35,000 ha in 1979, most
of which has very low grain yields. (Hainan still has to
import 225,000 tons of grain each year.); (4) the lack of
coal which leads to the use of wood as fuel. On the average
each person burns 1.5 kg per day, and with a population of 5
million people, this means that 2.7 billion kg of wood is
burnt every year - which corresponds to 4,000 ha of forest.
The average grain yield is only somewhat over 2,250 kg/ha.
For the clearing of mountain slopes investments are extremely
high (15,000 *yuan* per ha), and the production is very low (in
1979 rice yield was only 2,600 kg/ha).
His proposals for improvement of the ecological balance
were:

(a) New tropical forests. Protective forest belts should be
set up on mountains, plains and around cities and
villages.

(b) New rubber plantations, to be set up carefully. With regard to water and soil conservation, it would be necessary to construct level fields.

(c) Between the rubber trees, pepper, tea or coffee should be planted because these crops are profitable (especially pepper), and employ people.[40]

At the conference on the use of China's tropical resources it was suggested that the area of rubber plantations in Hainan be extended from the present 200,000 ha to 350,000-400,000 ha, so as to make China self-sufficient in natural rubber. However, opponents stressed the negative effects on plant life and wildlife and said that the wood of tropical forests might be more valuable than rubber trees.[41]

It seems that until now the natural advantages of Hainan have not been exploited. In view of the successful experiences of the neighbouring Leizhou Peninsula, reforestation should be very possible.[42] The tropical resources of wood, rubber, medicinal herbs, etc. promise to be more rewarding now and in the future than the low-yield foodgrain. Labour-intensive crops such as tea could be expanded, and processed for export. Hainan should follow the Taiwan example and use its geographical location for developing harbours, industry and trade. Employment then could be found along the coast, and slash-and-burn farming in the interior might be stopped. If China was unable to provide the capital and skilled manpower needed for such a qualitative change, foreign participation might be attracted. The present exploitation of the interior threatens to damage agricultural undertakings of the future because of soil erosion, loss of humidity and increased vulnerability to droughts and floods.[43]

The question posed at the beginning about foodgrain cultivation has been answered differently for the six areas discussed above. The general conclusion might be, however, that in marginal areas its acreage should be reduced as much as possible. Reforestation, green fertilizer crops and animal husbandry seem to be, even if less rewarding in the short term, more beneficial and economical in the long term. From the national point of view, there is a grain shortage which is made up by imports of about 10 million tons a year - which means a serious drain on foreign exchange. But animal husbandry still is underdeveloped in China, and has good export potential.[44] Moreover, the shortage of timber and fuel is just as serious as the grain shortage, if not more so, and the denudation of upstream areas has been shown to have very negative and costly effects downstream.[45] Furthermore, timber prices are expected to rise in the future, both within China and in the international market.[46]

Generally, timber stands in China are poor. Of the forestry reserves only one-half to one-third is considered usable. Since 1977 the average yearly decrease of forest resources has been 110 million cubic metres, almost 40 million cubic metres more than annual growth. About half of the decrease is due to regular timber exploitation.[47] The pace of felling is quickening, and there is a real crisis of resources. A major cause is the energy shortage: there is not enough fuel for household use or for village factories, so the villagers just have to go out and log trees and cut grass, or use plant stalks as fuel. This, of course, reduces fertility of the soil. According to a recent article,

> The rural population needs 540 million tons of plant fuel a year, which equals almost 300 million tons of standard coal - half of our country's production. But the stalks and wood are also needed as fodder, fertilizer or industrial material. Therefore only 300 million tons of stalks may be used as fuel. The State delivers some coal to the villages, but very little. 40 per cent of the peasants have a serious fuel shortage. The only short-term solution seems to be *biogas*. In 1979, there were 6.6 million biogas tanks, but only half of these were really usable. They have been extended too fast, without regard for quality or good management. This should be a lesson!
>
> Also, the peasants should plant forests for fuel, and the State should plan to supply more coal. In 1985 we should reach the minimum standard so that each peasant can have hot meals every day. In 1990 we should reach the level of 100 kg of coal per peasant.[48]

For other uses, such as paper, the future needs for timber will grow rapidly as well. The Government, however, has not given enough support to the maintenance of forests. Both the general shortage of coal and the closing down of many small coal mines (especially in South China) during recent years had the foreseeable effect of aggravating the onslaught on forests. These small coal mines were closed down due to their high production costs (yuan per ton) which were about twice those of the large mines. However, *external* costs were not taken into consideration, and I think this decision was a case in which departmental planning disregarded the needs of other sectors. The increased supply of rural electricity from small hydro-electric power stations, and biogas, has made no substantial contribution to the solution of the shortage.[49] State investments in forestry went down from 2 per cent of total State investments during the 1966-70 period to 1.35 per cent during 1976-80, and to only 1 per cent in the 1981-5 Plan.[50] In 1979 the Ministry of Forestry

was re-established, and a Forestry Law was promulgated with
overtly strict stipulations (e.g. Article 29, 'If collectives
want to fell more than 10 cubic metres of timber a year, they
have to ask permission from the county . . .') but with no
sanctions or organs of control. In fact, since then the
situation has gone completely out of control. According to
the same law, 'whether owned by the State or owned by a
collective, scenic forests, protective forests, water and
soil-erosion protection forests, old forests and precious
forests must all be managed by the State in a unified
manner'. However, in most cases the management of forests
was essentially handed over to the production teams. Different provinces made different regulations and nobody seems to
have bothered much about the law since then. Indiscriminate
felling had been very serious in 1958, after the formation of
the People's Communes; in the period after 1968, when foodgrain cultivation and self-sufficiency were stressed; and
since 1978.[51] The individualization of production under the
new responsibility systems introduced recently by the Government cannot but weaken control and management of forest resources further.

Much more successful has been the Government's policy of
stimulating tree planting along roads and near villages (a
common goal is 100 trees per inhabitant). Although trees
often compete to some extent with agricultural crops, they
also serve to reduce wind velocity, improve the microclimate, supply fuel to the villagers and strengthen embank-
ments of roads and canals. The most extensive and still
sustained effort, only partially successful, has been the
creation of a shelterbelt along the southern edge of the
Inner Mongolian desert, meant to stop the desert sand from
encroaching on the pastures and farmland of the loess
plateau and other parts of North-west China. Altogether
China has built 8 million hectares of protective forest
belts.[52]

Apart from the forests and fuel, and the protective belts,
there has been a rapid growth of orchards during the past few
years, stimulated by the greater economic freedom granted to
the farmers.

Plantations of chestnuts, walnuts, tea oil, *tong* oil, mul-
berry, and tea do not generally compete with foodgrain or
other crops, as they are usually planted in hillsides. The
total area of orchards now amounts to 8.3 million hectares,
and certainly will be expanded further, as they provide cash
income to the farmer. Intercropping of these plantations
with low crops which cover the bare soil (or, in the case of
chestnuts, with grass), may help to improve water and soil
conservation, and improve the microclimate as discussed in
the Hainan example above. One should be very careful, however,

in removing the original vegetation. The coastal areas in
south-east and south China especially, should develop such
export crops because of good climatic conditions, much un-
used hilly land, and access to foreign markets.

Official data state that during the three years, 1978-81,
the area sown for grain has been decreased by 7 million ha,
yet grain output rose by 15 million tons.[53] This suggests
that grain cultivation was abandoned primarily on low-yield
fields or under disadvantageous conditions. For the last
few years, official policy has supported diversification of
production instead of a one-sided stress on grain. The
policy formulation emphasizes the importance of a 'comprehensive development of agriculture, forestry, animal husbandry, sidelines and fishery'. How long this trend might
continue is ultimately dependent on foodgrain output and the
national or local demands for self-sufficiency in grain. It
is not easy to see, however, how local governments can influence grain output directly, as decisions on crop allocation have been taken out of their hands now and the manipulation of grain prices still is a prerogative of the
national government. The margin caused by moving away from
self-sufficiency in grain is often very small, as there is
not much commodity grain available - in 1979 only 14.7 per
cent of the total production. Most of this does not enter
the national market.

> As for grain, the provinces must be the units. They
> must be largely self-supporting. Only Hunan province
> exports 3 per cent of its grain production, other pro-
> vinces just 1 per cent. We must import from other
> countries grain, cotton and oil crops. It is rational
> to import grain and to raise cotton and edible oil pro-
> duction.[54]

This view was prevalent in 1980 but has been called into
question since then. A very interesting proposal was made
to concentrate State investments and efforts on China's
'middle zone' of farmland, the plain areas with irrigation
facilities but still with mediocre and unstable grain yields
(some 23 million ha); in the north-west there should be
mainly 'state ecological capital construction'; in the south,
forestry and tropical crops should be developed.[55] The State
Agricultural Commission proposed to strive for a foodgrain
output of about 400 kg per capita in the year 2,000, and to
build large commodity grain bases in the north-eastern provinces, the middle and lower Yangzi river region, and to
transform the Huang-Huai-Hai region into a cotton/oil crops/
foodgrain production centre. Others saw solving the problem
of grain shortage and the establishment of a socialist
modernized agriculture as opposite goals in the short-term.

A more orthodox Maoist position was that 'China is backward and cannot change quickly . . . problems facing China are insufficient grain, energy shortage, a deteriorated environment, and unemployment' - the order seems significant.[56]

These policy statements are all well and good for planners in Beijing, but do not come to grips with many of the problems we have seen to exist in the six examples discussed above. If anything, one would expect from a socialist planned economy the ability to foresee and protect the long-term interests of its population and economy, and to act on them. However, the political system does not seem to be able to stop continued destruction of the natural environment by short-sighted farmers. The laws enacted recently for forest protection and for environmental protection have been ineffective not only because of the lack of penalties for individuals and village authorities, or because of the lack of governmental control, but also because of objective factors - the fact that poor peasants, with little education, have to live off too small an acreage of farmland in a very vulnerable natural environment. One cannot expect the peasant to have an eye for long-term interests, or to have consideration for the 'external costs' their behaviour might cause. What is needed is a massive effort on the part of the Chinese government, to provide

- material incentives for local environmental protection efforts,
- supplies of coal or other forms of energy to the villagers,
- the construction of roads to areas which might be re-afforested or planted with orchards,
- education, directly, through local government, and through the Communist Party,
- effective penalties for offenders against the Forestry Law and the Environmental Protection Law,
- wider discretionary powers for county authorities to establish conservation zones where lumbering and re-clamation is forbidden, and to limit the number of cattle, sheep and goats,
- supplies of seeds, seedlings, and chemical fertilizer for afforestation areas and pastures,
- research on the optimal use of water resources, forest protection, soil improvement, and plant protection.
- subsidization or resettlement of villages where a major part of the economic activities are particularly harmful to the natural environment.

In the final analysis only rapid industrialization is able to create alternative employment and income opportunities for the Chinese peasantry and thereby diminish the pressure on land and nature.

Zhongguo Nongye Nianjian 1980, Nongye Chubanshe, Beijing 1981, p. 2. The under-reporting of farmland is due to several factors: evasion of rules concerning the extension of private plots, the tendency to strive after high unit yields in reports to higher authorities, and laxity or wilful delay in reporting reclamation of wasteland and clearing of forests. Also, the distinction between farmland used for fodder or green fertilizer crops and pastures may not always have been clearly made.

'The ecological balance and agricultural development', by Wang Gengjin, *Nongye Jingji Wenti* 1981 no. 6.

The number of commune members was 807 million. State farm workers totalled another 4.8 million, and State forestry farm workers 0.5 million, *Zhongguo Nongye Nianjian 1980.* The *total* agricultural population constituted 84.6 per cent of China's population (in 1978), *Jingji Kexue* 1980 no. 1, p. 8.

During the period 1949-77, 13.3 million ha were used up for State capital construction projects, 10 million ha for rural construction, and 3.3 million ha became wasteland or pasture; altogether the farmland area was reduced by 31.1 million ha, according to *Nongye Jingji Wenti* 1981 no. 1, p. 47. Reservoirs have taken up 2 million ha, ibid. 1980 no. 9, p. 61.

Nongye Jingji Wenti 1981 no. 1, p. 47.

This shows in the low yields of State farms, which produced 3 per cent of China's grain output in 1980. A notable exception is the 1.9 million ha of reclaimed lake areas along the Yangzi river, which are highly productive, Ma Hong and Sun Shangqing (eds.), *Zhongguo Jingji Jiegou Wenti Yanjiu,* Shijiazhuang 1981, p. 151.

In 1980, 4 million ha of farmland were marshy, 6.7 million ha saline, 9.3 million ha desertified and desiccated, 6.7 million ha subject to serious soil erosion; 12 million ha was low-productive red soil, *Zhongguo Nongye Nianjian* 1980, p. 2. China had about 35 million ha of farmland with grain yields below 1,125 kg/ha, *Nongye Jingji Wenti* 1981 no. 6. In 1977, 40 per cent of China's farmland was deemed low-productive, *Nongye Jingji Wenti* 1981 no. 1, p. 47.

8. According to *Zhongguo Jingji Nianjian 1980* from 1950 to
    1959, each year less than 20 million ha were struck by
    disaster; and during the six years 1972-77 each year an
    average of more than 33 million ha were struck. Disaster
    is usually defined as output being lower than 70 per cent
    of normal.

9. 32 per cent of China's farmland was considered to be
    highly productive in 1977, *Nongye Jingji Wenti* 1981 no.
    1, p. 47.   There are 25.3 million ha of wet rice fields,
    and 22.4 million ha of irrigated fields, *Zhongguo Nongye
    Dili Zonglun,* Beijing 1980, pp. 75-9. Of the latter,
    4.5 million ha are irrigated by pump wells, the remainder
    by surface water, *NCNA* Chinese 27 July, 1978.   42 per
    cent is mechanically ploughed, but only 10 per cent
    mechanically sown, *Beijing Home Service* 14 Oct., 1979. If
    we assume that chemical fertilizer is only used in irri-
    gated areas, then the level of application almost trebled
    between 1972 and 1979, to some 1,200 kg (20% N) per ha,
    Zhongguo Nongye Nianjian 1980.   Cotton is grown almost
    exclusively in the irrigated areas of North China and of
    the Middle and Lower Yangzi Region.   For the productivity
    of grain areas, see the map of county averages in 1971,
    Zhongguo Nongye Dili Zonglun, map 4-1, and E.B. Vermeer,
    China, Koninklyk Instituet voor de Tropen (Royal Tropical
    Institute), Amsterdam 1982, p. 56.

10. See e.g. E.B. Vermeer, 'Comment', *China Quarterly* no. 81
    (March 1980) on grain yields in Shandong in 1956 and
    1978.

11. Ma Hong and Sun Shangqing (eds.), *Zhongguo Jingji Jiegou
    Wenti Yanjiu,* p. 500.

12. Ibid., p. 526. Capital construction, communications and
    utilities employed 5.8 million people; commerce, finance,
    science and culture 7.8 million people.

13. The State invested 47.3 billion *yuan* (1 *yuan* equals
    about US$ 0.50) in water conservancy capital construction
    and 29 billion *yuan* in water conservancy work expenditure
    during 1949-79, *Zhongguo Nongye Nianjian* 1980, p. 25.
    Local self-paid investments in water conservancy were 50
    billion *yuan, Nongye Jingji Wenti* 1981 no. 2, p. 4.
    State agricultural investment figure from *Nongye Jingji
    Wenti* 1980 no. 8.

14. The estimate was made by Wang Renzhong for the average county of Wugong in the Wei River plain, Shaanxi, *Zhongguo Nongye Nianjian* 1980 p. 172.

15. For reclamation and salinization problems in Xinjiang since 1949 see E.B. Vermeer, *Water Conservancy and Irrigation in China; social, economic and agrotechnical aspects*, Leiden 1977, p. 206-10.

16. Zhu Zhenda, 'Problems concerning the development and utilization of the interior of the great Taklamakan desert', *Dili* 1961 no. 4, pp. 156-7, 192; Nongye Chubanshe, *Zhongguo Nongye Dili Zonglun*, Beijing 1980, p. 96.

17. Han Qing, 'On the deterioration of the water quality in the Tarim basin and its control after reclamation', *Dili Xuebao* vol. 35, no. 3, Sept. 1980.

18. See O.J. Todd, *Two decades in China*, Peking 1938; Huang Wenxi, *Soil and water conservation of the Yellow River Basin*, Yellow River Consulting Board, Studies on the Yellow River Project no. 5, 1947; Teng Tzu-hui, *Multipurpose plan for controlling the Yellow River and exploiting its water resources*, Beijing, FLP, 1955, for the early period. The average annual silt content of the Yellow River (Huanghe) is 36.5 kg per cubic metre at Shanxian, which is located where the Yellow River enters the North China Plain (i.e. upstream seen from Nanluohe). This is about 100 times the average silt load of the Xijiang in Guangdong.

19. Li Xueceng, *Huangtu Gaoyuan*, Beijing 1960; *Huanghe Zhongyou Dichu Shuitu Baochi Shouce*, Beijing 1959; Zhao Mingfu's comments on the Yellow River Middle Reaches Water and Soil Conservation Conference, *Shuili yu Dianli*, 1965 no. 6 (Dec.) pp. 6-11; and articles in *Renmin Ribao* 26 Nov., 1978 and *Guangming Ribao* 3 Jan., 1979.

20. E.B. Vermeer, 'Income differentials in rural China', *China Quarterly* no. 89, March 1982, pp. 1-33.

21. Wang Gengjin, 'The ecological balance and agricultural development', *Nongye Jingji Wenti* 1981 no. 6.

22. From 1970 till 1976, the State provided 13 million *yuan* in relief funds, and bank debts amounted to 10 million *yuan*. In 1978, per capita collective income was only 29 *yuan*. From 1970 to 1977 a total of 600,000 tons of

grain should have been paid in tax; instead, the State
had to supply the county with 250,000 tons of grain.
Wang Gengjin, 'The Ecological balance . . .', and
Guangming Ribao 3 Jan, 1979.

23. '. . . Changes in the natural environment of the Sanjiang
plain, and its rational exploitation', *Dili Xuebao* vol.
36 no. 1, March 1981, pp. 33-45.

24. Nongye Chubanshe, *Zhongguo Nongye Dili Zonglun*, Beijing
1980, pp. 92-3.

25. According to *Zhongguo Nongye Nianjian* 1980, pp. 289-90,
which uses a larger definition of the Sanjiang Plain,
yearly precipitation during the 1975-80 period went down
to an average of only 300-400 mm per year. But for the
remainder of China this was a dry period as well, and
there is no connection between reclamation and dry
weather. As the Sanjing is a rather wet confluence,
there is no danger of its becoming a 'dustbowl'. It is,
nevertheless, concluded that the forests should be protected and increased to the Heilongjiang average, because forests reduce wind velocity and improve the microclimate.

26. In Beijing, ground water resources amount to about 3
billion tons annually, of which 2.6 billion are tapped
near saturation, Li Weiyao, 'Broad prospects for the
development of China's ground water', *Renmin Ribao* 28
Nov., 1981.

27. Zhu Laidong, 'The water of Tianjin', *Dili Zhishi* 1982.

28. The Northern half of the North China plain has the most
severely polluted surface water in the whole of China,
Zhang Li Cheng and Dong Wenjiang, *Huanjing Kexue* Vol. 2
no. 5 (Oct. 1981) pp. 71-4, map.

29. Zhu Laidong, op. cit.

30. *NCNA* 21 Aug., 1978; *Shandong Provincial Station*, 15 Jan.,
1982. There are no details on how the silt problem will
be handled.

31. Hubei originally had 870,000 ha of lakes, but only
200,000 ha were left in 1980, *Zhongguo Nongye Nianjian*
1980, p. 213. The Dongtinghu Lake in Hunan was reduced
from 700,000 ha in 1870 to 435,000 ha during the 1950s.
According to Ma Hong and Sun Shangqing, op. cit. p. 151,

in the six provinces along the Yangzi river 1.9 million
ha of lake surface were reclaimed until 1980.

32. *Renmin Ribao* 5 April, 1979.

33. T. Woldai and W.B. Vermeer, 'Geomorphology and Land Use
of the Jianghan Plain and surroundings, from Landsat
imagery', *ITC Journal* 1979 no. 4.

34. 'Reclamation of lakes, more losses than profits',
Zhongguo Nongye Nianjian 1980, pp. 238-9. But other
sources indicated a larger acreage, *NCNA* 4 May, 9 Nov.
and 23 Dec., 1961.

35. See E.B. Vermeer, *Water Conservancy* . . ., pp. 311-14;
'Has the silt load of the Yangzi river increased or not?'
Nongye Jingji Wenti 1980 no. 12; *Xinhua* 19 Sept., 1980.

36. 'Reclamation of lakes, more losses than profits',
Zhongguo Nongye Nianjian 1980, pp. 238-9.

37. Ibid. pp. 27-9. This was due also to newly built dams,
industrial water pollution, agricultural pesticides etc.

38. *Dili Zhishi* 1982 no. 3, p. 14.

39. Yu Dechang, 'Some ideas on the control of the deterioration of the ecology of Hainan island and the establishment of a new ecological system', *Nongye Jingji Wenti*
1981 no. 11, pp. 49-53.

40. Ibid.

41. *Zhongguo Nongye Nianjian* 1980, p. 283. Together with
the expansion of rubber trees in Xishuangbanna and elsewhere to a total of 230,000 ha, China might then produce
550,000 to 700,000 tons per year. For a short description and map of China's natural rubber see *Dili Zhishi*
1982 no. 7, pp. 4-6.

42. Since the fifties Leizhou Peninsula almost trebled its
forest cover, to 23 per cent of its surface area in
1980, *Dili Zhishi* 1982 no. 1, p. 25. This had favourable
effects on climate and production. Li Keliang, 'Forest
Construction in Leizhou Peninsula', *Nongye Jingji Wenti*
1982, no. 8, pp. 23-35.

43. (Cont'd). For present developments in Hainan, see *China
Trader* March 1981, pp. 50-73.

44. Foreign exchange earnings in 1979 from exports of live-
    stock products totalled 1.53 billion *yuan;* agricultural
    products 6.96 billion *yuan;* processed agricultural pro-
    ducts 11.85 billion *yuan, Nongye Jingji Wenti* 1981 no.
    11, pp. 10-17; *Zhongguo Nongye Nianjian* 1980, pp. 331-2.

45. This point has been stressed recently after the serious
    floods in the Yangzi river basin in 1980 and in Sichuan
    and Shaanxi in 1981, by He Xiwei. 'Has the silt load of
    the Yangzi river increased or not?', *Nongye Jingji Wenti*
    1980 no. 12, pp. 49-52, and 'A discussion of the relation
    between forests and water conservancy, after the flood
    damage in Sichuan', ibid., 1981, no. 12, pp. 3-8. It is
    shown that districts with a good forest cover suffer much
    less damage from rainstorms than those with little
    forest. In a controlled experiment, reforestation of a
    barren mountain led to a reduction of run-off by 70 per
    cent, and of silt by 99 per cent. Lowest and highest
    flow of the Minjiang river in Sichuan became much more
    extreme since the forest cover of its basin was reduced
    after 1949 by almost one-half, to 19 per cent now.
    During the 1975 floods in Henan two major reservoirs
    with a very weak forest cover in their upper reaches
    collapsed, while other reservoirs stood. Part of He's
    arguments were refuted in *Dili Zhishi* 1982, no. 5.

46. Kong Fanwen, 'A discussion on forest value and the
    Theoretic Price of Timber in China', *Linye Kexue* 1982 no.
    2, pp. 177-84.

47. Timber stands average 79 m^3/ha in China, as against a
    world average of 110 m^3/ha. Of its forestry reserves of
    9.5 billion m^3, only 3.5 billion m^3 is considered to be
    usable. Yearly timber exploitation is 50 million m^3,
    according to *Zhongguo Nongye Nianjian* 1980, p. 16.
    Another source states that the volume of forest re-
    sources is 8.6 billion m^3, of which one half is available
    for logging, and that the actual logging volume comes to
    over 200 million m^3 per year. Per inhabitant China has
    only one-eighth of an hectare of forest, against a world
    average of 1 ha. Timber growth per ha is only 1.84 cubic
    metres, as against 3.1 in Japan, and 5.5 in West Germany,
    Wang Gengjin, 'The ecological balance and agricultural
    development', *Nongye Jingji Wenti* 1981 no. 6.

48. Ma Hong and Sun Shangqing(ed.), op. cit. p. 286. In
    1978 the level of coal consumption for household use was
    61 kg per capita in rural China, and 409 kg per capita in
    urban China, ibid. p. 277. See also Rong Donggu 'The

relation between energy consumption and national development', *Jingji Yanjiu* 1980 no. 6, pp. 49-55.

49. Small hydro-electric power stations have been under
    political attack since 1979. In 1980, they supplied
    11.9 billion kWh or 37 per cent of total rural use. Half
    of their capacity was created during 1975-9, at a State
    investment of 1.3 billion *yuan, Renmin Ribao* 17 Feb.,
    1981.

50. Li Zhankui e. a., 'Quickly change the passive situation
    of concentrated over-felling of the forests in our
    country's main forest areas', *Nongye Jingji Wenti* 1982
    no. 1, pp. 9-12.

51. 'The changeover from large collectives to small collec-
    tives may fit the present level of agricultural pro-
    duction forces, but after the authority over forests was
    turned over to the production teams . . . again the
    forests suffered large-scale destruction', *Nongye Jingji
    Wenti* 1981 no. 1, p. 7. In some provinces such as
    Yunnan, a premium of 750 *yuan* per hectare was given for
    reclamation of forest or wasteland. For each hectare
    which was afforested a premium of 3 to 15 *yuan* was
    given, *Zhongguo Nongye Nianjian,* 1980, p. 217.

52. *Zhongguo Nongye Nianjian* 1980, pp. 2, 162-3.

53. *Xinhua* Domestic Service 31 Dec., 1981.

54. Ma Hong and Sun Shangqing op. cit., pp. 143, 159.

55. Weng Yongxi e. a. 'Views on strategic problems in China's
    agricultural development', *Jingji Yanjiu* 1981, no. 11,
    pp. 13-22.

56. 'A discussion about agricultural development strategy at
    the Beijing Conference of the Chinese Agronomy Society
    (26 Feb., 1982)', *Nongye Jingji Wenti* 1982 no. 4, pp.
    50-4. The last view was put forward by Liu Zhideng of
    the Academy of Agricultural Sciences.

How do economic and political reforms affect people's individual existence? What is the emotional response to ideological change and how do external social conditions influence feelings and mental outlook?

To try to find an answer to these questions the natural thing would be to turn to literature and art as an obviously important source of information. It is therefore regrettable that it has not been possible to include in this book any article dealing with recent developments in Chinese literature, even though this subject was discussed at the Sandbjerg Symposium. The following broad outline of some trends within the field of literature should thus be read as a cursory supplement to the six proper articles that make up this book.

Literature reflects change in a much more subtle and indirect way than do policy statements or statistics. By focusing on the subjective response of individuals to society and environment it shows the spiritual change that accompanies or precedes the implementation of far-reaching political decisions, or other major events in a given country. This is the way we are used to looking at Western literature, and the fact that we are now able to see contemporary Chinese literature as fulfilling this function is in itself a symptom of change. Formerly literature in the People's China used to reflect change in a very direct and crude manner, appearing like fictional illustrations of prevalent party policy towards a given field - be it agriculture, industry, education or class struggle and ideological behaviour - rather than elaborations of a personal experience of the complex reality. But now it would seem that the role of literature in China has approached that of literature in the West, even if there are, of course, still important differences. For one thing, despite liberalization, party interference in literature is still something to be reckoned with. Moreover, to the majority of Chinese writers literature is still much more of a moral/political exercise involving a strong sense of obligation and responsibility towards the state than it is to the majority of their Western colleagues.

Writing a survey of major literary trends is no longer as easy as it was back in the late sixties and early seventies. Then it sufficed to mention a few keywords like 'worker, peasant, soldier, positive superhero, bright ending' (*guang-ming de weiba*), and to add a summary of the latest articles in *Hong Qi* (Red Flag) in order to provide a perfectly adequate description of the overall literary output. Now, fortunately, it would be impossible to present a full picture of the extraordinarily complex, and in some ways creatively contradictory, literary scene, and no such attempt shall be

made here. As this book is concerned not just with change as
it can be registered in numbers, statistics or organizational
reforms, but also with implications of change, I shall limit
my considerations to some new directions that can be di-
stinguished from earlier changes.

The developments in literature since the fall of the Gang
of Four and up to 1984 can be divided into four periods. A
gradual diversification began very slowly in the first period,
late 1976 to mid-1977, which was characterized by a literature
that looked a lot like that of the previous years, except for
a reversal of the roles of hero and villain. Then at mid-1977
the publication of Liu Xinwu's short story, *Class Teacher,*[1]
marked the beginning of the next period, a period which could
be designated as 'controlled taboo-breaking', when more and
more hitherto forbidden zones were trespassed.[2] From the
beginning of 1979 came the time of truly controversial literature. This third period represented the high point of so-
called 'exposure literature' and 'scar literature', lasting
through 1980.[3] That year also marked the beginning of a more
widespread concern with artistic technique, which till then
had only existed in the unofficial literary magazines and in
the contributions of a few officially publishing writers.[4]
This was to continue also after the Party, by early 1981,
managed to curb what was considered rampant social criticism
in the form of literature. During the last period, from 1981
onwards, the situation seems to have stabilized in a climate
of relative openness and tolerance, despite campaigns and
attempts by the Party to regain the upper hand. In any case
the climate is certainly extremely liberal if compared to any
other period of the PRC before 1979.[5]
The themes in the most controversial part of the literature of the past seven years read almost like a catalogue of
social evils: corruption, prison camps, backdoor-ism, cadre
malpractices, arbitrary political decisions, overcrowded
housing, the hard lot of middle-aged intellectuals, the lost
generation of the Cultural Revolution, broken relationships
between parents and children, and stories of love and divorce.
But despite the great variety in subject matter, most of
these stories seem to share a common underlying theme: the
conflict between the inner emotional needs on the one hand,
and the demands arising from society's norms and the collective ideology on the other. Indirectly, there is an overall
awareness of the hypocrisy or disintegration of social norms
and values, but at the same time the high personal costs or
the impossibility of breaking these norms.

The general atmosphere of disintegration and unpredict-
ability which pervades this critical 'exposure' literature

of especially the last three periods, provides the background
for the elaboration of the psychology of the individual, the
exploration of the human mind, which can be found in what is,
in my opinion, the most trail-blazing trend in contemporary
Chinese literature: I am referring to the trend towards an
abandonment of the traditional narrative structures of
(socialist) realism, in favour of an introspective, *subjectivist* kind of literature. This implies the use of the
limited point of view instead of the omniscient view of the
narrator of the realist tradition. Even though a limited
point of view has been employed by May Fourth writers such
as Lu Xun and Yu Dafu, it has been conspicuously absent in
most literature of the People's Republic.[6] Thus it can be
said that this subjectivist trend, though not necessarily
quantitatively dominant, represents an even more radical
break with the literary tradition of the last thirty years
than does the 'exposure' literature in itself. Even if the
writing of this recent period has been more courageous and
of wider scope than ever before, the 'exposure' literature
nevertheless takes up a tradition of the Hundred Flowers and
other liberal periods. One might say that the subjectivist
literature, in terms of the very *technique* it uses, has
drawn the structural conclusions from the objective conditions of life as revealed by the 'exposure' literature.

The best-known example of a writer pursuing such new
techniques is of course Wang Meng, now a member of the
Central Committee. Much has been written about his work,
both in China and abroad. Many of his stories published
between 1979 and 1982 are characterized by the use of a kind
of stream-of-consciousness as a vehicle for rather uncontro-
versial subject matter.[7] Some of them are quite successful
and there is no doubt that his example has helped new ways
of writing to become more widely accepted, just as his work
has furthered the move away from a heavily normative kind of
literary criticism, obsessed with content and message, towards a more descriptive, interpretive one, taking into
consideration language and artistic method.

Wang Meng was not, however, the first Chinese writer to
open new paths, stylistically. Examples of a very high
quality can be found in the periodicals of the Democracy
Movement, above all in *Jintian* (Today), artistically the most
outstanding of these.[8] The works found here, published from
the end of 1978 to early 1981, but some actually going back
to the mid-seventies, combine an innovative, original form
with a deeply disturbing content. Stories by Zhao Zhenkai[9]
and Chen Maiping,[10] together with some of the best poetry of
this century by Zhao Zhenkai (Bei Dao), Shu Ting, Gu Cheng and
Mang Ke, mark the true beginning of a literary trend which

came to exert a strong influence in the following years. The above poets became the focus of the heated and prolonged debates over what was termed 'obscure' poetry (*menglongshi*).[11] Their experiments with language as part of an existential search, their unorthodox juxtaposition of disparate images, though clearly unintelligible to many older writers, can be seen as part of an attempt to recreate a lively, meaningful language, out of what had been for so many years in the service of politics. Actually a modern case of '*zheng ming*', a rectification of the language, to make the denotations correspond to a reality beyond that of political jargon and cliches.

In fiction the subjectivist tendency became noticeable, especially from late 1979, not only with those who consciously turned towards this mode of expression. It is also traceable to writers who are not primarily associated with an experimental form, such as, for example, Liu Xinwu, by the ample use of interior monologue and psychological description.

On the basis of both its formal characteristics and inherent attitudes, some of this literature comes very close to what in the West is termed the *modernist* literary tradition. Modernism in the West is generally held to be the literary expression of the collapse of a unified world view, which began to be felt by the mid-nineteenth century. It is no coincidence that the period of high modernism came in the years following World War I. The general cultural and spiritual climate at that time shows similarities to that of post-Cultural Revolution China. It is therefore quite understandable that literary modernism has been the main topic of discussion in literary circles in China during the last four years, and that works by Western modernists such as Kafka and Virginia Woolf have been objects of fascination and emulation among young Chinese writers.[12]

One particular group of writers deserves our special attention: the women. Never before in the history of Chinese literature has there been such a wave of talented female writers. I need here only mention such names as Zhang Jie, Zhang Xinxin, Zhang Kangkang, Shen Rong, Zong Pu, Ru Zhijuan and Wang Anyi. Their works constitute an extremely significant part of the literature of the eighties. Not unexpectedly the bulk of their writings belongs precisely to the subjectivist category. The sensitive, emotional angle being one traditionally ascribed to women, it is only natural that the emergence of a true feminist literature should coincide with a general subjectivist trend in literature. Some of their stories are heavily autobiographical, notably those of Yu Luojin, whose *A Winter's Fairy Tale* and *Spring Fairy Tale* sparked wild criticism as well as immense curiosity when they were published in 1979 and 1982.[13]

It is interesting to note that the Chinese feminist literature, alongside issues that have become obsolete in Western literature, e.g. the fight to marry for love, contains some of the same basic conflicts that are also reflected in Western literature written by women. In broad terms it is the same kind of conflict we see in a lot of other contemporary Chinese stories - the conflict between inner dreams and the demands of society - often manifesting itself in the impossibility of combining an emotionally fulfilling love life with an intellectually fulfilling work life. This is the theme of such different stories as Shen Rong's *At Middle Age*[14] and Zhang Jie's *The Ark*.[15]

The Ark, published in 1982 in the influential Shanghai journal *Shouhuo* (Harvest), tells the story of three single women, two divorced and one separated, who live together. This story, together with Zhang Xinxin's *The Dreams of our Generation*,[16] published four months later in the same magazine, and Zhang Kangkang's *The Northern Lights*[17] from a year earlier, are in my opinion among the most interesting and artistically successful examples so far of the new Chinese women's literature. All the female main characters in the three stories can be said to be outsiders, in the sense that they have felt the need for something 'more' than the ordinary daily life can provide according to the officially accepted social conventions. Zhang Jie's characters, however, have consciously broken the written and unwritten rules for proper female behaviour, and are trying to establish an alternative lifestyle.[18]

In contrast to Zhang Jie, both Zhang Kangkang and Zhang Xinxin resort to myths or fairy tales in order to present the dilemma. For Zhang Kangkang's protagonist, who is searching for the right man at the same time that she is seeking to understand herself, the northern lights, something fantastic and beautiful which she has never actually seen, become a metaphor for a different and truer life. Hans Christian Andersen's tale, *The Snowqueen*, is often referred to in this story, as is another tale of his, *Thumbelina*. The latter tale about a tiny girl who gets betrothed to a mole, thereby gaining material security but forever denying herself the pleasure of sunlight, has been seen by Chinese women writers as a forceful image of women's fate in marriage. This theme also appears, together with other Western and Chinese fairy tales, in Zhang Xinxin's story.[19] (For a Dane it is interesting to note the influence of Hans Christian Andersen on a number of young Chinese writers, including Wang Anyi and Gu Cheng.)

The issues raised in the women's literature, concerning the marriage system and the plight of women, have been subjects of sharp debate in the Chinese press. Already in 1979, Zhang Jie's controversial short story, *Love must not be Forgotten,*[20] set off the first penetrating discussions of love and marriage since 1949, focusing on the rights of the individual, and the repression of feelings resulting from the impact of both socialist and traditional morality. This rather sentimental story has a message which is extremely radical in the context of Chinese society, where most marriages are still either arranged by others or based exclusively on social convenience: it is better not to marry at all than to marry someone you don't love.

The women's literature (as well as other literature dealing with existing problems), therefore, serves a double function: as literature in its own right and as a catalyst for public debate. It is one of the characteristics of the People's Republic that public debate on social issues is conducted primarily in the form of debates around works of literature. This is one thing that has not changed. It is always safer to argue indirectly, in terms of fictional characters, than to venture personal opinions directly on a touchy subject.

This function, of course, also makes the literature under discussion very vulnerable to attack, and all the four stories mentioned above were strongly criticized during the so-called 'anti-pollution' campaign lasting from late 1983 to early 1984.

This 'anti-pollution' campaign looked very frightening at the time, and was reminiscent of pre-Cultural Revolution campaigns to purge writers and wipe out poisonous weeds. Yet in a paradoxical way, this campaign, like the one against Bai Hua in 1981, seems more to illustrate the change *away* from the old all-embracing pattern. The heavily condemnatory statement against modernism, existentialism, humanism, irrationalism, etc., did not really seem to have any long-term or wide-ranging effects. And even during the campaign, the writers criticized continued to publish, and controversial pieces appeared in, for instance, the Guangdong based magazine *Huacheng* (Flower City).[21] Whatever the factional political reasons for starting the campaign, probably it was not really an expression of the Party's wish for complete control. Rather, it indicated the Party was willing to tolerate a certain diversity of opinion, but feared the emergence of a truly alternative literary milieu bearing its own set of aesthetic criteria and standards of evaluation.

Another reason for literature's new, relative independence from party politics, compared to the pre-Cultural Revolution

period, is the reorganization of the system for publication.
Since 1980 publishing companies are no longer dependent on
centrally-approved plans for publication, and their success
is largely determined by their economic profit. The trend
towards a decentralized system of publication, in connection
with a general market-oriented economy, means that literary
periodicals have attained a high degree of economic independence and responsibility, which makes it quite difficult for the contents to be controlled centrally. There is
a fierce competition among different publishing houses, while
the sheer profusion of publications makes tight control
impossible. [22]

The gradual reform of the publishing industry, together
with the general change in the spiritual climate resulting
from the political and cultural upheavals, the increased
status of intellectuals, and the diversification of the
readership, have all contributed in creating a more multi-
faceted perception of the writer's role in Chinese society.
It would seem that writers as a whole are no longer perceived
of as an integrated part of the establishment to the extent
that they were before the Cultural Revolution. Most Chinese
writers have always been fundamentally loyal to Party and
State. The conflicts and purges, though involving deviating
views on the role and contents of literature, were more part
of factional struggle within the party than a question of
punishing dissident writers. [23] Earlier it was very difficult, if not impossible, to become a fairly well-known
young writer without being caught up in and totally absorbed
by the official system. But now a number of promising young
writers are able to get their works published in some of the
numerous periodicals without having become part of the
cultural apparatus - even though they themselves might wish
to become so. Thus, while some middle-aged writers, after
having broken new ground in style or themes, may now seem to
have joined the establishment, there are still quite a few
popular and interesting younger writers around who, in the
eyes of their readers, take a more independent stand.
Writers in China still command a tremendous respect and
influence and get a response to their work which their
Western colleagues can be envious of. The traditional respect for the master of the written word, together with the
recently regained May Fourth role of the writer as a fighter
for justice, combine to make these younger writers objects
of admiration and fascination as well.

There are many striking similarities between contemporary
literature and the May Fourth literature of the early
twenties. The subjectivist, individualist tendency, then as
now, can be regarded as a consequence of strong reactions

171

against norms and ideology. The May Fourth revolt against
Confucian ideology is now being paralleled by (or combined
with) the revolt against Maoist puritanism and insistence on
unquestioning Party loyalty. In the general atmosphere of
change, hitherto dominant moral and social conventions begin
to lose their validity as standards for behaviour and judgement. As in the twenties, love and marriage have become
important issues. And, like sixty years ago, the impact of
and interest in Western literature are strong. Just as the
Westernized syntax and idiom of the May Fourth pioneers
alienated large groups of potential readers, so the modernist
technique of some present-day writers is not immediately
palatable for the average reader. Finally, the generation
gap is again an undeniable fact, which acts as a dynamic
force as well as posing serious problems for the leadership.

Yet such similarities should not lead one to overlook
important differences in the functions and content of
literature then and now. For one thing, whereas May Fourth
literature was the outcome of a general nationalistic
awakening and a broad cultural movement, the present
literature can still to a large extent be seen as a reaction
against a political movement of a rather more contradictory
and sinister kind. Hence the difference in tone and outlook.
Also the belief in the importance and power of literature in
transforming China and making it rich and strong, is hardly
as firm among the writers of today as it was among their
predecessors.

But whatever the similarities and differences, the May
Fourth heritage is very much present on the literary scene
today. There is a clear move away from the previously
dominating Yanan heritage, towards the May Fourth heritage,
the other mainstream in modern Chinese literary traditions.
With the May Fourth heritage rehabilitated, the contemporary
Chinese writer can now choose between at least three different roles, or a combination of the three: the traditional
one, as a loyal servant to the state, contributing to the
four modernizations; the dangerous one, as a fighter for
social justice; and the recently-added one, as a writer in
search of existential truth, using literature as a means of
probing the human condition.

Anne Wedell-Wedellsborg

1. 'Ban zhuren', *Renmin wenxue,* 1977, 11.

2. I.e. literature of that period, incl. 'Class Teacher',
   often seemed to be more or less faithful reproductions
   of new official policy towards specific problems. See
   Anne Wedell-Wedellsborg: 'Det Onde ligger i fortiden'
   Basar Oslo 1980, 3.

3. See for instance Perry Link ed.: *Stubborn Weeds,* Indiana
   1983; W.J.F. Jenner: '1979: A New Start for Literature
   in China?' *China Quarterly* no. 86, 1981; Perry Link ed.:
   Roses and Thorns: The Second Blooming of the Hundred
   Flowers in Chinese Fiction 1979-80, Indiana 1984; and
   Howard Goldblatt ed.: *Chinese Literature for the 1980s,*
   New York 1982.

4. Notably Wang Meng, see below. For the unofficial maga-
   zines, see Flemming Christiansen, Susanne Posborg, Anne
   Wedell-Wedellsborg: *Den demokratiske bevaegelse i Kina,*
   Copenhagen 1980. German edition: *Die Demokratische
   Bewegung in China,* Munich 1981.

5. It has been generally argued in Western articles on the
   post-Mao literary scene that the years 1979-80 constitute
   the truly liberal period, and that since 1981 literature
   has become much less controversial and therefore much
   less worthwhile reading. While it is true that the truly
   sensational and critical 'exposure' literature is now
   hard to come by, this does not in my opinion mean that
   literature has become less fascinating. Interesting and
   relevant stories have been published during the last few
   years. Disturbing and unorthodox stories such as Zhang
   Jie's 'The Ark' and Zhang Xinxin's 'The Dreams of our
   Generation' (see below) belong to this period. See also
   David Goodman: 'The Short Story and its political Context: To write the word for "man" across the Sky', paper
   presented at the Cologne Workshop on Contemporary
   Chinese Literature, April 1984. To be published.

6. It has, however, been occasionally used by writers such
   as Fang Ji and Ru Zhijuan.

7. See for instance Phil Williams: 'Stylistic Variation in
   a PRC Writer: Wang Meng's Fiction of the 1979-80
   Cultural Thaw', *Australian Journal of Chinese Affairs,*
   Jan. 1984; William Tay: 'Wang Meng, Stream-of-conscious-
   ness, and the Controversy over Modernism', *Modern Chinese
   Literature,* vol. 1 no. 1, 1984 and Wang Meng: 'An Open

Letter on Stream-of-consciousness', *Modern Chinese Literature,* vol. 1 no. 1, 1984.

8. See Christiansen, Posborg, Wedell-Wedellsborg 1980 and 1981.

9. For an introduction to Zhao Zhenkai's fiction see Bonnie S. McDougall: 'Zhao Zhenkai's Fiction: A Study in Cultural Alienation', *Modern Chinese Literature,* vol. 1 no. 1, 1984. For an analysis of one of his stories see Anne Wedell-Wedellsborg: 'Chinese Modernism?', paper presented at the Cologne Workshop on Contemporary Chinese Literature, April 1984. To be published in: Helmut Martin and Wolfgang Kubien (eds.): *Cologne Workshop 1984 on Contemporary Chinese Literature.* Cologne 1985. For a translation of stories see Zhao Zhenkai: *Waves,* translated by Bonnie S. McDougall and Susette Cooke, The Chinese University Press, Hongkong 1985.

10. Pen-name Wan Zhi.

11. Bonnie S. McDougall: *Notes from the City of the Sun,* Poems by Bei Dao. Cornell East Asia Papers. Ithaca, New York 1983.

12. Anne Wedell-Wedellsborg: 'Chinese Modernism?', see note 9.

13. Yu Luojin: 'Yige dongtian de tonghua', *Dangdai,* 1980, 3 and 'Chuntian de Tonghua',*Huacheng,* 1982, 1. See also Emily Honig: 'Private Issues, Public Discourse: The Life and Times of Yu Luojin', *Pacific Affairs,* vol. 57, no. 2, 1984.

14. Shen Rong: 'Ren dao zhongnian', *Shouhuo,* 1980, 1.

15. Zhang Jie: 'Fangzhou', *Shouhuo,* 1982, 2.

16. Zhang Xinxin: 'Women zheige nianji de meng', *Shouhuo* 1982, 4.

17. Zhang Kangkang: 'Beijiguang', *Shouhuo,* 1981, 3.

18. See also Yue Daiyun and Carolyn Wakeman: 'Women in Recent Chinese Fiction - A Review Article', *Journal of Asian Studies,* vol. XLII no. 4, 1983.

19. See *Zuopin yu zhengming,* 1983, 8 for a discussion of Zhang Xinxin's story.

20. Zhang Jie: 'Ai shi bu neng wangji de', *Beijing wenyi*, 1979, 1.

21. Also Gao Xingjian's controversial modernist play 'Chezhan' (*Shiyue*, 1983, 3), first performed in Beijing in June 1983; was again performed in November the same year.

22. Hans Hendrische: 'Das Publikationswesen nach 1977', paper presented at the Cologne Workshop on Contemporary Chinese Literature. To be published.

23. Bonnie S. McDougall: 'Writers and Performers, their Works and their Audiences in the First Three Decades', in McDougall ed.: *Popular Chinese Literature and the Performing Arts in the People's Republic of China,* University of California 1984.